Creative Alchemy

**Accessing the Extraordinary
Power of the Muse
to Transform Your Art
& Your Life**

Victoria Fann

The Human Alchemy Project
Asheville, NC 28801

Copyright © 2018 by Victoria Fann

All rights reserved.

No part of this book may be reproduced in any form or by any electronic or mechanical means, including information storage and retrieval systems, without written permission from the author, except for the use of brief quotations in a book review.

Cover art painting and design and title page design by Liz Labunski. The painting on the cover is called *InSink*. Her artwork can be found at https://labunskistudio.com/.

CONTENTS

Introduction   v
Acknowledgments   xi

PART I
Gather the Courage   3
1. Resistance and Procrastination   7
2. Response-Ability   13
3. Express the Inexpressible   18
4. Ego Games   23
5. Breaking Free   28

PART II
Honor Your Muse   37
6. Unlearning   41
7. Tuning In   47
8. Making Friends   51
9. Caring and Feeding   57
10. Priorities and Boundaries   62

PART III
Light the Creative Fire   69
11. The Power of Imagination   73
12. Creative Juice   78
13. Sacred Space   83
14. Creative Rituals   89
15. Daily Practice   92

PART IV
Listen to Life   101
16. Dreams   104
17. Signs and Signals   108
18. Intuition   112
19. Body Wisdom   118

20. Nature's Medicine   123

PART V
Find Your Voice   129
21. Permission to Love Yourself   133
22. Quantum Leaps of Being You   140
23. Seize the Moment   144
24. Become the Vessel   149
25. Fate and Destiny   153

PART VI
Transform Your Life   159
26. Creative Dates   162
27. Creative Community   166
28. Sharing Your Work   171
29. Service to Others   176
30. Keeping the Faith   180

Conclusion   187
About the Author   189
Creative Story Contributors   191

INTRODUCTION

WELCOME CREATIVE SOULS!

I'm so glad you have decided to take this creative adventure! There are many steps that happened along the way to make this book possible. The first was the Creative Alchemy Meetup Group that I co-facilitated in Seattle from 2011 to 2012, which provided the inspiration and skeleton for this book. Following that came the Creative Alchemy ecourse that put the meat on the bones and breathed it into life. The benefit to you is that you have the energy of all the creative souls who came before you, infusing this book with their wisdom, inspiration, and love (and a few of their creative stories).

Before we begin, let's pause here for a moment. This is a good time to set an overall intention for what you'd like to receive at the completion of this journey. First, listen to your heart. Check in with yourself to see what you need right now. Second, give yourself permission to ask for it full out. Finally, take a deep breath and as you do, make space for the precious gifts available to you deep within.

This book is a special opportunity to cultivate a more

authentic and heart-centered creative practice, which is in alignment with your Muse and taps into your true and original Voice. Nothing less than that will suffice, nor will it be sustainable.

HOW TO READ THIS BOOK

1. Relax and enjoy each moment of the book as it's unfolding. Savor it like a good meal.
2. Really engage with the chapters. Read them several times so that you can gain the most from their subtler messages.
3. Pace yourself. Don't push or force anything. While opening up some of the cabinets and drawers of your consciousness, you may find some things that surprise you, delight you, or bring up old, buried feelings. Allow these things to come and allow yourself the time and nurturing to process all of it. With awareness comes great freedom. With vulnerability comes a new level of bravery and trust. With honesty, comes a lightness of being as you shed the heavy burdens of denial.
4. Be extra kind and loving to yourself. Check in frequently to see how you're doing—add a little pampering to your routine, talk with a trusted friend, journal, spend time in nature, etc. Mostly, give yourself the space to open part of your creative life that you may not have really examined before.
5. Most of all, celebrate each step you take that brings transformation into your life and touches the lives of others.

RECOMMENDED SUPPLIES LIST

To get the most out of this book and the activities at the end of each chapter, please gather the following supplies:

1. Journal or notebook
2. Favorite pen
3. Colored pencils
4. Pretty stationary and envelopes
5. Three mason jars with tops (plus anything you might want to use to decorate them)
6. Candles
7. Incense
8. Favorite essential oil scent
9. Inspirational music
10. Smudge stick
11. A few favorite sacred objects
12. Inspirational piece or pieces of art

LETTER TO YOURSELF

Take a piece of that pretty stationary and write a letter to yourself sharing your intention for this part of your creative journey. Focus on what you would most like to receive from this experience. Put it in an envelope, address if to yourself and tuck it away to read when you have finished the book.

MY STORY - WHY I'M SO PASSIONATE ABOUT MY MUSE

I've been in love with writing and words since I was a child, lost in the magical world of books. A refuge and sanctuary from the complexity of my daily life, I enjoyed how easy it was to be transported into a whole new reality just by reading the words on a page.

Creativity had a major presence in my extended family. My grandfather on my father's side was a classical composer and his wife, my grandmother, was a painter, sculptor, and poet. Her mother was also a poet. My father wrote music also, but he was drawn more to country music. Dance was the central focus of my mother's life from the age of three. Her mother made all of her costumes while she performed on stage and on a local television show. She was advised by one of her teachers to move from Cincinnati, where she grew up, to New York to study with Martha Graham. Instead, she ended up pregnant with me, ending her dance career, following my father to the suburbs while he pursued a career as a jingle writer.

Being exposed to such an emphasis on art, music, and dance, and growing up with a strong appreciation for reading (both parents were avid readers), I couldn't help but feel a nudge in the direction of the arts. My mother insisted that I take piano lessons the way she had as a child, so I initially tried to make music my creative medium. I took lessons from a long line of teachers. In high school, I practiced piano for hours, added voice lessons and joined a 200-member chorus that performed Handel's Messiah in Carnegie Hall and Avery Fisher Hall. In college, I even studied flute for a semester, but my heart wasn't in it; it wasn't flowing.

So I quit.

I realized it was time to get honest with myself. Having published some of my poetry in my high school literary magazine and written lots of in-depth papers for my classes, it became clear to me that in addition to my interests in psychology, philosophy, and consciousness, writing was where I would find my greatest joy.

The sudden death of my father when I was twenty-one, marriage at twenty-three, and a baby at twenty-four turned my world upside-down. Creativity was still a major focus, but instead of being at the center of my life, it was relegated to the gaps in between my work and parenting duties.

Besides not having enough time, my biggest issue creatively was finishing projects. Ideas poured through me like a fountain, but capturing them, containing them, and molding them into finished projects always seemed to elude me. I did manage to get some short articles and essays published, however, I struggled to take on and manage larger projects. Unfinished books of short stories and essays, along with novels, plays, and screenplays lay in piles on my desk, in folders in a filing cabinet, and in files on my computer waiting for me to craft them into a form that was accessible to others.

Along the way, I decided to get some support. I started a writing group called Mothers Who Write in 1989. This created one of the biggest openings in my creative life. As I gathered with other writers twice a month, I found my confidence soaring and my commitment to my writing expanding. Finally, there were other people in my life that cared whether I finished something. I loved the feeling that I was not alone. Becoming a cheerleader and friend to other writers was incredibly enlivening—it added joy and color to every aspect of my life. I felt that I had stumbled upon one of the key ingredients for a creative life. Many groups and writing classes evolved from that first group.

The second, and perhaps even bigger breakthrough in my creative life happened many years later. I'm not sure exactly how it happened, or the specific moment, but what I do remember is a period of time when something just clicked. Perhaps my Muse felt sorry for me, perhaps she was tired of waiting, or perhaps I'd reached a critical convergence of ideas and number of hours invested in writing combined with an undying passion for the creative process. Whatever it was, a door opened and out of the blue, I felt myself let go. My need to control fell away and I found myself tapping into something much larger than just me. It felt as though a Divine Presence stepped in to help, not only with inspiration and ideas, but also with the actual execution of these ideas into forms that had structure, and yet flowed out onto the page.

The creative process shifted from a place of strain and struggle to effortless collaboration. A weight was lifted when I discovered I simply had to show up and get out of the way, letting the work flow through me. This way of creating permeated all aspects of my life including my coaching practice, the classes I taught, the groups I facilitated, and whenever I spoke in public.

It was as though I'd stumbled onto a big secret.

Over time, I learned the importance of honoring this relationship with my Muse by treating my creative life in a sacred way. It was my desire to share this discovery that lead me to write this book.

Working with my Muse, the creative process took on a much larger scope. I began to see a connection between my creative life and my spiritual life. My Muse created a natural bridge between these two aspects of my life. Now I see them as a continuous, seamless circle that draws from the same Source.

In addition, my problem with finishing projects stopped being an issue. Working in partnership with my Muse elevated my confidence enough to push through most of the resistance, or fear that came up. I no longer tried to control or lead the process, but rather trusted the greater intelligence enough to follow it where it wanted to go.

Taking the control away from my ego and handing it over to my Muse also allowed me to remove any attachment I had to the outcome of my work. This freed me up to simply enjoy the journey, rather than focus only on the results of my efforts. It's the alchemy of creativity at its best: a catalyst that uplifts, frees, and transforms you into that authentic soul, expressing yourself authentically as only you can.

What more could any creative spirit want than that?

Now it's your turn. It's my intention that as you travel through these pages, you'll access and deepen your relationship with your Muse.

Now…take a deep breath. Let's begin!

ACKNOWLEDGMENTS

I am full of gratitude and appreciation for the support I've received in bringing this book into form. It's been a long journey with lots of twists, turns and bumps. I've learn so much along the way. Blessings and hugs to all of you who encouraged, funded, edited, guided, nudged and most of all, listened to me when I was overwhelmed, frustrated and full of doubt. A special nod to all the beautiful, creative women whose stories appear in these pages. Finally, thanks to my Muse, whose gifts uplift and sustain me, and without whom this book would be only a fleeting idea taking flight across the ethers.

PART I

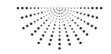

GATHER THE COURAGE

GATHER THE COURAGE

Nature loves courage. You make the commitment and nature will respond to that commitment by removing impossible obstacles. Dream the impossible dream and the world will not grind you under, it will lift you up. This is the trick. This is what all these teachers and philosophers who really counted, who really touched the alchemical gold, this is what they understood. This is the shamanic dance in the waterfall. This is how magic is done. By hurling yourself into the abyss and discovering its a feather bed. — Terrence McKenna

When we least expect it, life sets us a challenge to test our courage and willingness to change; at such a moment, there is no point in pretending that nothing has happened or in saying that we are not yet ready. The challenge will not wait. Life does not look back. A week is more than enough time for us to decide whether or not to accept our destiny. — Paulo Coehlo

IT TAKES DISCIPLINE, COMMITMENT, AND PERSISTENCE TO complete a creative project. It also takes inspiration, passion, and *a whole lot of courage*. Courage to keep going when we want to quit. Courage to show up when we don't feel it. Courage to work through the saboteurs of fear, interruptions, distractions, resistance, and procrastination.

Where does this courage come from?

Mostly, it comes from merely being brave and doing what feels so daunting and difficult. Getting support helps. Having a creative habit helps. Being madly in love with your project helps. Having your Muse as your best friend helps. But sometimes, it just takes a whole lot of willingness to fail, to do it wrong, to do it badly, get rejected, and so on, trusting that eventually things will turn around, and that through the sheer practice of showing up and doing it, you'll get better, your projects will get better, and you'll stop caring so much about what other people think.

To create takes courage, and it's absolutely worth it!

I could stop here, but I won't because there's so much juicy stuff to cover in this section. In building this beautiful foundation for you and your Muse, we've got to get into some of the mucky stuff, the not-so-pretty aspects of the creative process. Perhaps then, you'll see why you've been blocked or resistant in the first place, or you'll have some clarity about why some projects flow and others don't at all. One A-HA moment will be worth a stretch of messiness. While you're digging around in the shadows, a light will come on making sure what was dark will never be hidden again. This will free you up to be creative in brand new ways! How cool is that?

In this section, we're going to peel back the layers and expose our excuses, laziness, and overall procrastination. We'll also look closely at our fear and resistance to see how they play a role in our self-sabotage.

But that's not all. We're going even deeper than that. We'll explore the shadow side of creativity—not something many of us examine too often. This is the terrain of the ego, or more accurately, the hidden ego, that motivates us to do things for approval, to please others, to get love or attention. We like the identity of artist, writer, actor, musician, etc. For some people that's the primary reason they create art. They don't want to write a book; they want to have written it with all the alleged glory that comes with it. No joy in the process for them, but only in the end result. So, we're going to take a look at how the ego likes to hijack our creativity for ulterior motives and rob us of the simple joy of creating.

All of us have a creative comfort zone and limiting beliefs that keep our creativity safe, but at the high price of restricting it. We're going to venture outside of that zone for a bit to look at how we may be consciously or unconsciously holding ourselves back from that remote wilderness of the creative unknown. We may discover that we're afraid to be or express ourselves as we really are.

A bit challenging to be sure, but the rewards will be well worth the effort.

Are you ready?

REFLECTION QUESTION

Are you holding yourself back and if so, what limiting beliefs keep you from pulling out all the stops?

BEFORE WE BEGIN

- Set an intention for this section.
- Write a list of limiting beliefs that are holding you back in your CA journal.
- Find a role model in the arts whom you consider to be brave and whose work you admire because of its originality and the raw courage it took to create it and share it with the world.

1
RESISTANCE AND PROCRASTINATION

> Every creative person, and I think probably every other person, faces resistance when they are trying to create something good...The harder the resistance, the more important the task must be. — Donald Miller

> Resistance cannot be seen, touched, heard, or smelled. But it can be felt. We experience it as an energy field radiating from a work-in-potential... Its aim is to shove us away, distract us, prevent us from doing our work. — Steven Pressfield

EXCUSES ARE AS CONTAGIOUS AS THE FLU. TO IMMUNIZE OURSELVES we need good strategies and tools. Because there always seems to be a reason why we can't get to our creative projects, and ironically, many of those reasons sound really convincing. But in the end, excuses leave us feeling out of touch with this part of our lives, and out of touch with ourselves.

During those dry times, it can feel as if your Muse has abandoned you, leaving you wondering if, or when, she'll return (more on this later). Sometimes the source of this resistance is related to a specific project. Maybe the energy's not there, something's missing or more research is needed. Sometimes a life circumstance or relationship distracts you for a while, interrupting your momentum and making it difficult to re-enter the process. Other times, your resistance may involve a deeper creative crisis. You may be paralyzed with fear or huge heaps of doubt and an extreme lack of confidence. Perhaps you were criticized or rejected and don't feel that your work is good enough, or matters to anyone.

The War of Art, by Steven Pressfield, is a powerful little book, and the concepts in it are incredibly simple. The whole book boils down to this: *the only enemy in the way of creating art is resistance.* Resistance takes many forms; many of them are insidious and sneaky, but this enemy is what lies behind all our excuses and reasons why we're not doing our art.

It is comforting to know that we're not alone in our struggles with resistance. Learning to recognize it for what it is begins to break up the seemingly solid inertia so that you can move again. Once you see that you're deliberately avoiding any creative activity, just stop. Observe what's happening. Acknowledge it. Then see if you can identify what the resistance is about. Is it a legitimate reason? Or is it a big fat excuse to keep you from the discomfort of facing some of the doubt or fears surrounding a creative project?

Often, it's our old friend, *excuse*. And if excuses are contagious, we need a remedy. We'll be exploring a variety cures throughout this book, but before we do, we need to look at procrastination, the darker sibling of resistance.

PROCRASTINATION

Procrastination is what happens when resistance gets the upper hand and we're stuck in the thick mud of inertia, unable to move forward for days, weeks, months, and sometimes even years. Projects lay collecting dust—abandoned, lifeless, and without hope. We can see them every day without even acknowledging them, until finally we don't remember why we ever felt excited about them. We become disconnected from our passion because it's easier; life is less complicated, we tell ourselves. Passion is messy and it stirs up too many feelings. I'm just fine the way I am, thank you very much.

But the truth is we're not fine. Not at all. Because an essential part of who we are has been locked away. Our pilot light is a mere flicker of what it once was. We're operating at a diminished capacity and don't even realize it. We've joined the living dead. Comfort has replaced passion. Meeting our obligations is our prime concern now. Then once met, our attention is on relaxing and forgetting about those obligations—an unending cycle of monotony that lulls us into a zoned-out place in which we are existing, but not living.

There's no way around it: creativity needs passion; we need to fall in love again with our dreams.

Love will move us forward with far less effort than discipline alone.

It's not all work. Plus, if we're not enjoying the process, then we shouldn't be doing it. The process is the heart of it. That's where the juice lives. What we're seeking is a fine marriage between passion and discipline.

∼

CREATIVE STORY BY TANYA COLE

"As an artist, mum of three boys, wife, occupational therapist, and creativity coach, time is of the essence, and yet I seem great at wasting it through resistance and procrastination. I am frustrated when mundane, everyday commitments and tasks prevent me from being at my easel. However, when I finally do have the time to be there, I find myself doing other things such as sitting at the computer. I play Russian roulette with the minute hand on my clock until it starts getting dicey with the hour hand as well. "Will I or won't I get over to my easel?" I ask myself. My left-brain ego-mind has EVERYTHING to do with it. It hampers and sabotages my intuitive, creative, and infinite possibilities right brain at every turn.

I have done this dance for a few years now. But in the last few months, the game is up and my left-brain ego is the loser. You see, I've caught it in the act. I've been observing its tactics from over in my right brain. When I am in the flow, creating, I remind myself to view myself from my left brain for a moment and see where the resistance is occurring: why I procrastinate, why I avoid, and why I create so much internal struggle for myself.

The answer was two-fold and it was this: 1) I wasn't really taking myself seriously enough; I was allowing my fear of success and fear of failure to have a little tête-à-tête party with each other, knowing full well that I could always jump tracks back into my old job and live life like everyone else—a tad dissatisfied and a fair bit bored. It was familiar and effortless, even if undesired by my heart. In short, I hadn't fully committed to my artist's path and I was just dabbling. So time WASN'T of the essence, that's why I was wasting it. 2) I hadn't had the deep, running-through-my-veins-with-desire conversation with the universe; nor was I really showing enough gratitude for being able to have the luxury of dabbling towards my big childhood dream.

These two things changed once I got deeply, deeply honest with myself around commitment and gratitude. I decided I HAD to take the *plunge because my husband had the meter running (I would have to take up a regular job half an hour away in the next town from January 2016, putting the kids in after school care; which would effectively reduce my creative time to 'not very much at all.' IF, I couldn't make it as an artist/art facilitator). I made a choice. Rather than spend money to go on a holiday, I committed close to $3000 towards further learning as a Creativity Coach. My art career trajectory was set the minute I signed up to make those payments for the course. The other thing I did was to make a commitment to the Universe and those around me. Each night when I go to bed, I silently ask, "Universe. Please show me how I can serve you." I also give gratitude for my life and thank myself for the path I put myself on. In the mornings, I say thank you for my night's restoration and for my day ahead. Then I set the intention that it will be a good day.*

It's working; the universe is delivering. I am too busy doing what I love, to want to resist (because I consciously chose it and so did my purse) or avoid it, and I am keeping my left-brain ego up against the wall on any further, sly manoeuvres. It might change, but it's what has worked and is working for me right now."

Then there are our inner demons, whose sole job is to fill us with self-doubt, spinning us out with thoughts such as: "Who am I to think I have anything worthwhile to say?" "What difference does it make if I do this or not?" "This is no good." "I don't have time." "Nobody gives a damn." There's nothing worse for an artist than letting these creepy, dark parasites get the upper hand. You've got to cut them off at the door, block their entry, disarm them with a firm, protective stance. Denying they exist will only make them stronger. Face them as you would a salesman at your front door —kindly say you're busy, and not interested in what they're selling. Then close the door and go back to work.

If you're having a particularly bad day, I recommend a technique that outsmarts them every time. Just quit. Give up and say to yourself that you're never writing another word, painting another stroke, or playing another note. Go to bed, watch television, play computer games, but don't do anything creative. Protest, sulk, complain. Full out. Take it to the max. The next day, you'll be surprised to discover that after a day of complete rebellion, you can return to your projects with enough energy to complete a mountain of work.

What about beautiful days, outings with friends, and other seductive attractions? How do we handle those? With discretion. We need to meet our commitment first, then we can play. Our lives should be balanced enough to accommodate a healthy mix of work and pleasure. There are always exceptions, of course. But beware of the tendency to make too many exceptions and sabotage your progress. Then you'll be right back where you started.

Question: How do resistance and procrastination affect your creative life and what is the cost (i.e. stress, poor health, physical symptoms, spiritual or emotional dis-ease)?
Activity: Make a list of typical ways you sabotage your creativity. Make a list of ways you let the world/others sabotage you.
Inspiration: Watch Seth Godin's *Quieting the Lizard Brain* on Vimeo or YouTube

2

RESPONSE-ABILITY

Each of us has the right and the responsibility to assess the roads which lie ahead and those over which we have traveled, and if the future road looms ominous or unpromising, and the road back uninviting-inviting, then we need to gather our resolve and, carrying only the necessary baggage, step off that road into another direction. If the new choice is also unpalatable, without embarrassment, we must be ready to change that one as well. — Maya Angelou

Responsibility is what awaits outside the Eden of Creativity. — Nadine Gordimer

YEARS AGO, WHILE STILL NAVIGATING THROUGH THE WILDERNESS OF parenting, I faced many of the same issues that Tanya shared in the previous chapter. I'd get overwhelmed by the ongoing demands on my time. Life felt full, but often chaotic with too many hours spent repairing cars, raking and mowing the lawn, weeding the garden, shoveling the sidewalks and driveway, cleaning the house, washing and folding the laundry, buying food, clothes, and presents, filling out forms, paying bills and taxes, answering e-mail and phones, helping with homework, arranging playdates and sleepovers, and so on. It was a never-ending to-do list. I used to wonder how I could even begin to think that I had the energy or space to write. During those times, I often spend so much time recovering from all the to-dos that I rarely took a moment to even ask myself what I wanted. Here's a little rant I wrote then ... I'm sure many of you can relate:

> "My dreams seem to be passing me by, a slow train filled with passengers who know where they're headed, are happy to be together, and confident they will arrive on time. I stand on the edge of tracks wondering how I missed the connection. Air hits me in gusts as car after car whizzes past, the people inside unaware of me except as part of the scenery, because where they are going is important. In fact, they are stuffed to the brim, overflowing with their own self-absorption, which is why, I suppose, I cannot join them. My thoughts have been captured by the needs of others; I've willingly allowed myself to be taken prisoner by them, surrendering without a fuss, protesting only occasionally when the whim strikes me.
>
> My house is too crowded, there is no place for my Muse to relax or settle in. She simply stops by once in a great while, knocks on the door, peeks in, shakes her head at the mess, and tells me she'll come back another time.
>
> I talk about writing all the time, and it makes me feel like a fraud. I'm not a writer. Rather, I'm a bottom feeder in the world of artists: I teach, I run a couple of successful writers' organizations, I prostitute my talent by working as a copywriter, and worst of all, I talk about wanting to write. A wannabe. Remember that game Chutes and Ladders? Well, I've landed on the largest slide in the game and slipped nearly back to the beginning. I'm still brushing myself off and wondering how in the hell I got here. I'm floating adrift on the daily barrage of family and

work details; the flotsam and jetsam clogging my creative arteries, until I can hardly breathe. "

My issue was never writer's block. Far from it. For me, it was because I always feared the floodgates in my brain would open up and I wouldn't be able to catch the ideas fast enough to make use of them. My writer brain was a leaky dyke that I dealt with by jamming the holes with my neglect and refusal to play.

Instead, I wrote a lot in my head. While walking, or driving, or standing in line, a ticker tape of brilliant ideas for essays, book titles, and screenplays ran through my head. I'd hear entire paragraphs recited in a steady stream, at least, that is until I got distracted by physical reality, such as having to cross a busy street or place an order for lunch. It amazed me how much stuff was going on in the background of my life.

I did my best to hold this background hyperactivity at bay. It got quiet when it didn't think there was a chance in hell I'd pay any attention, such as in the middle of a family crisis or when I was sick. At those times, it faded into a subtle whisper. However, as soon as I even cracked the door open a little bit, it roared back into my life again, bold and dramatic. When I stole little bits of time to write, my writer brain became excited like a dog waiting to be taken for a walk or a child on a warm summer evening that wants to stay out and play. Thinking the door was finally open, it threw ideas my way, hoping I'd catch them. It was very self-centered that way, and wanted lots of undivided attention, something I was in short supply of then. Just as I'd get settled in and comfortably into a rhythm, something in my "real" life interrupted me, taking me away from my writing for long periods of time, making me lose track of what I was doing in the first place.

How about you? Do you react to life or do you respond?

. . .

There's a big difference between the two. Reacting is more of a "putting out fires" approach. To react is to act out, to jump in when being called forth through an outer invitation to act. Responding, on the other hand, is more grounded, centered, and conscious. Responding involves tuning into the present moment and acting in a way that reflects your inner values. It is done with mindfulness and awareness of the Highest Good for all in that moment. Personal agendas are put aside in favor of a win-win approach.

How do you see your ability to respond to both your inner and outer experiences and directives?

The way we interact with both our inner and outer worlds is an indicator of our ability to respond to each as needed. Sometimes we respond appropriately; sometimes we don't. Either way, we need to own it and act accordingly.

In our creative lives, responding to the competing needs of our daily lives can be greatly helped by learning to respond more often to the whispers and nudges that come from intuition. This way, we can find harmony between the inner and the outer. Rather than letting the outer world direct our every action, we can tune in, thus, adding our own voice and needs to the mix. Responding to our inner direction also shifts the way we move through our outer world. Our decisions will inevitably be quite different when they resonate with our inner values.

Developing our ability to respond touches all aspects of our lives and shapes our world. Harmony is a sign that both our inner and outer worlds are working in sync, rather than at odds. Disharmony is a sign that we need to respond differently—sometimes it means something needs to change.

It took many years, lots of support, and heaps of determination to make the shift from reacting solely to the external demands around me to responding to the inner callings of my heart, which I is how I discovered the voice of my Muse. I sometimes mourn the time I lost spinning around in circles, driving myself crazy with frustration.

WHAT ARE YOUR CREATIVE SABOTEURS?

- Not enough time
- Not enough money
- Not enough information
- Not enough skills
- Not enough self-confidence
- Not enough persistence
- Not enough daily work toward goals

Question: How can you take more response-ability for your creative life?
Activity: Work on the all the questions in this chapter and then look at some ways you can shift the way you respond to your inner guidance and the way you respond to the outer world. See if the way you respond to both the inner and outer has any impact on your creative life.
Inspiration: *Inner Engineering: A Yogi's Guide to Joy* by Sadhguru

3
EXPRESS THE INEXPRESSIBLE

I found I could say things with color and shapes that I couldn't say any other way - things I had no words for. — Georgia O'Keeffe

Art is the triumph over chaos. — John Cheever

WHEN I WAS A TEENAGER, MY MOTHER TOOK ME TO A PLAY CALLED, *For Colored Girls Who Have Considered Suicide When the Rainbow is Enuf* by Ntozake Shange. We were so close to the stage, I could see the actors spit when they spoke. The energy was electric and edgy. I remember feeling awe over how courageous the writer was to speak her truth with such raw nakedness. It takes guts to be that real. It also requires us *to step way out of the socially accepted comfort zones of our culture* and risk being judged by family, friends, neighbors, co-workers, etc.

Creativity is sourced from within, requiring it to move through the filter of a human instrument—an instrument shaped and scarred by the wounds we carry from childhood into adult life. These wounds influence the way we relate to the world, and it is often through our creativity that we discover a channel to release these deeply buried secrets, mysteries, (and demons), so that they no longer have a hold on us.

Many famous creative minds experienced a major trauma in their lives that strongly impacted their artistic works. Creative expression is how they chose to process it and, as a result, others experiencing loss or trauma, were often touched by it.

How can we turn our creativity into a catalyst for healing and transforming our unexpressed shadows?

By illuminating them, honoring them, releasing them, and ultimately channeling them into our work. In this way, we not only give a voice to our own pain, but also touch the universal pain of others. Bringing our shadow into the light allows for its acceptance and healing. It doesn't mean that all creative expression has to be about our wounds, but in order to give full expression to who we are, we cannot bury, hide or ignore the parts of us we consider unpleasant. Instead, we can integrate these shadows into the full body of our work making our work deeper and more real. Others can feel this and will sense our courage and more likely resonate with our honesty.

Expressing the raw, uncomfortable, and what may feel inexpressible is a way of liberating the creative flow. Allowing our truth to arise unimpeded can remove obstacles, unblock resistance, heal self-doubt, and purge the emotions that keep us pent up. Repressed emotions and ideas don't go away. They just stay dormant. Sometimes they fester causing unease and pain. Better to free them. Release the prisoners so the genius within can shower the world with unique gifts.

Bringing what cannot be easily expressed from the invisible

into the visible can be terrifying, but it can also bring about a lightness of being. In the early stages of the creative path, many artists engage in creative projects associated with their family of origin. This can be a necessary step that opens doors to the rich, creative projects that will follow. It's good to honor those early biographical roots. Give them life. Share them. Use them to heal.

Then go deeper.

What emerges from that lush compost will encompass a broader, more universal viewpoint. The artist evolves to become a scribe for humanity—the work reverberating for far longer than the life of that particular artist. The intense universal art that lasts for generations carries a genius quality because the work comes from the subterranean well of the collective unconscious. You cannot access that if you're hanging out protecting your personal story or sticking to your comfort zone. The juicy stuff is in the realm of the unknown. It is transpersonal. It is beyond the world of the day-to-day. It is the kind of art, writing, music, theater, etc., that makes people feel as though the artist accessed something from a completely different world. It's the kind of creative stuff that blows people's minds because it's not of the mind—it's of the Greater Mind. It's transcendental. It's where the alchemy of creativity lives.

To get there, you need to open up ALL the stops!

Thankfully, your Muse will willingly help you with this. She'll guide you, and she'll even show you where to focus your energy. This is the land of Beauty and Love. This is where you can get into states of creative bliss and ecstasy. However, it's not for the faint of heart. Why? Because in this realm you cannot play it safe. You cannot try and control the expression. You are, in a sense, truly an instrument of the Divine; you are there to capture this amazing flow, filtering it through your open vessel.

AN OPEN VESSEL

To be an open vessel means being willing to do whatever it takes to treat yourself, your life, and your art in a sacred way. Honor it, respect it, and show up to receive what life wants to give you. If your shadow stuff is getting in your way, get some healing with a trained healing professional. By all means, don't deny or ignore it. Holotropic Breathwork is a powerful way to work with shadow energy in a safe environment. Bodywork is another way. Reiki and other healing modalities can help integrate chaotic energy. Then you can learn to channel the energy into your work in an integrated and healthy way.

The film director, David Lynch, makes very dark, though highly creative movies that are uncomfortable to watch. In interviews, he frequently mentions his daily meditation practice—something he hasn't missed in over thirty years. I'm sure this practice plays a significant role in his ability to enter these darker realms but still remain balanced. He's a great example of someone who's learned to work with this shadow material and turn it into unusual creative projects.

The artist, Alex Grey, has used many different types of hallucinogens to travel into the unseen worlds. The result has been art that reflects those realms and yet, his art is also grounded by his background in anatomical drawing. The blend of otherworldly and human gives it a universal focus.

There are many ways to become familiar with the inner worlds of the unknown and move into your creative practice in a way that's balanced. The point is not to avoid those worlds because of fear, but to find the best way for you to navigate there and receive the many blessings that await you.

Question: How do you integrate the shadow aspects or the inexpressible into your work?

Activity: Read a book, watch a movie, visit a gallery, see a play, listen to music of someone who crosses the barriers of the personal into the universal or transpersonal. Observe some of the subtler qualities of the work, and note your experience when engaging with it. Then see how you can expand your creative work a little by bringing more of the inexpressible and the hidden into your own work. Do something brave. Take a risk. Try something new. Use new tools. Work in a new location. Collaborate with someone on a new project. Even if it is only a baby step, move a little out of your comfort zone and notice how it impacts your own creative process.

Inspiration: Visit Alex Grey's Chapel of Sacred Mirrors website and view his art.

4
EGO GAMES

The mistake we all make is in thinking that certain standards exist and that we must meet these standards in order to establish our place in the universal hierarchy. But hierarchies in artistic expression are not valid nor universal; they're personal. — Madlyn Rhue from book, *Actors as Artists*

To prevent its annihilation, the ego forces us to be constantly on the watch for anything that might threaten the symbols on which it relies [for identity]. Our view of the world becomes polarized into 'good' and 'bad'... things that support the image of the self... and those that threaten it. This is how the third veil of Maya works: it distorts reality so as to make it congruent with the needs of the ego. — Psychologist Mihaly Csikszentmihaly from the book, *The Evolving Self*

ALL ARTISTS, REGARDLESS OF THEIR CREATIVE MEDIUM, STRUGGLE with ego issues. It's part of the territory of being human and it gets amplified in the realm of the creative. Many people who set out to create something don't give their egos much thought—they simply create. Ego issues usually make their appearance when we feel blocked and when we decide to share our work. Of course, these issues may show up at any stage in the creative process, but when we bring in the outside world either literally or in our head, we step into the realm of judgment, self-doubt, comparison, and all kinds of other goodies.

To put it simply: ego—or identification with our small self or personal story—inhibits creativity. The result is that we get stuck and our art becomes lifeless due to expectations, assumptions, limiting beliefs, conforming to social ideals and standards, people pleasing, fear of rejection, etc. This is the dark, often hidden side of creativity, which has grounded many projects, leaving many artists feeling empty.

True creativity is an opening to the invisible realms of the Higher Self—the vast collective unconscious where there is free access to total creative expression *without limits*. This realm is where the beauty and joy of original expression lives. Unfortunately, the ego loves to hijack the creative process, holding the artist hostage. It often plays on the deep insecurity and feelings of unworthiness of the artist, masking it with *an overinflated sense of specialness*, thus interfering with the artist's authenticity and true voice.

EGO ANTICS

Exposing the mostly undetected antics of the ego in the creative process can unleash us from its grip so that we may regain our creative footing. One way to approach this is to simply observe how you deal with ego or "small self" issues.

Another way to stir up awareness is to ask yourself some provocative questions:

1. How do you deal with the expectations and pressure to conform to social ideals and standards?
2. How do you handle the fear of rejection?
3. What's the motive and passion behind your creativity?
4. Can you be creative even if your creativity isn't witnessed by others?
5. How can you avoid vanity in the midst of your success?
6. Has your ego ever been the reason you did something creative?
7. What's the difference between ego-motivated self-expression and self-expression that comes from a deeper, egoless place? Do you know the difference? How do you personally access that deeper place?

Find a creative friend or two to share these questions with and discuss the answers. Or take some time and write the answers in your CA journal. You may be surprised at what you discover hidden just beneath the surface.

As you'll discover in Section 2 and subsequent chapters, cultivating a relationship with your Muse will become a major tool to help you move beyond the wants and needs of the small self or ego. Why?

The Muse simply won't tolerate the interference of the ego.

She wants you open and receptive to what she wants to gift you without all the consideration of the outside world—how it will make you look, what your friends will think, this isn't good enough, etc. She's not at all interested in those external criteria. Her focus is on the original creative flow as it is interpreted and then produced by your unique instrument. That is her mission and her task. What you do with it doesn't concern her. What concerns her is that you receive her gifts as they come with acceptance, love, respect, and gratitude.

Now, here comes the tricky part:

Do you have the courage to bring forth what you receive as it is, without trying to change it or fix it so that your small self looks good?

I'm not suggesting that you not revise or present your work professionally. What I am saying is to not let your ego fill you with doubt and scarcity, so that you give up on a big dream or sell out a big dream because someone offers you bundle of money, but asks you to make some major compromises as part of the deal.

Do you see where I'm going with this? If you spend lots of time cultivating your connection with your Muse—really refining your unique Voice—then you certainly don't want to back down under external pressure. Our egos can make us so worried that we're going to fail and be criticized and embarrassed, that we compromise our own integrity so that we'll fit in. But we end up empty inside.

THE HIGHER SELF

The work of your Muse is a gift to share with the world. It's not a commodity to make you feel worthwhile. It's not a prop for your identity. The ego just tends to find sneaky ways to trick you into producing beautiful things to feel loved, gain attention, and feel special. Never a good way to go! This is why you hear people say that creativity is hard work, because they're doing it for ego gratification—their Muse is long gone having hightailed it out of there fast. *Trust me when I say that your Muse wants NO PART in ego games.* She only works with those who are sincere about bringing the formless, timeless gifts into manifestation to add something of meaning and beauty to the world. Nothing less will satisfy her. Sure, she'll stick around while you fumble a bit to get your bearings, but if she senses your sincerity, she'll be right there to back you up, eventually doing most of the heavy lifting for you.

Watch that ego! Stay true to your inner guidance and you won't go wrong. This is the reason much of this book is focused on the Muse. She's your best ally against your ego and the pressure from the world. If you trust in this possibility, you may eventually discover that the world truly loves what you bring forth. But pleasing the external world won't be the reason your start out doing it.

Okay ... that's quite enough to absorb in one chapter. Take a deep breath and spend some time reflecting on this. It may take several weeks, or even months, to fully grasp the subtle ego stuff going on in your life. But if you commit to staying true to your integrity, you'll find your way.

Question: Does your ego ever hijack your creativity? If so, in what ways?
Activity: Reflect on the questions in this chapter and simply observe the way you relate to the world, specifically your creative world. Study your deeper motivations and see what you discover.
Inspiration: Read "The Ego and the Self" by Steven Pressfield on his website.

5
BREAKING FREE

Reality doesn't impress me. I only believe in intoxication, in ecstasy, and when ordinary life shackles me, I escape, one way or another. No more walls. — Anaïs Nin

The most important kind of freedom is to be what you really are. You trade in your reality for a role. You trade in your sense for an act. You give up your ability to feel, and in exchange, put on a mask. There can't be any large-scale revolution until there's a personal revolution, on an individual level. It's got to happen inside first. — Jim Morrison

HAVING THE COURAGE TO CREATE AND PUSH THROUGH ALL THE distractions and resistance along the way ultimately points to one thing: freedom. Rising above limiting beliefs and negative habits, moving into spaciousness and presence is a radical 180-degree shift for most of us. It's a long, arduous path that requires tenacity, patience, and deep commitment, but those who reach the summit rarely complain about what it took to get there. They're too filled with the exhilaration of having done it.

In the creative world, as in everyday life, your biggest competitor is yourself. We drag our feet in protest, falling into the human defaults of laziness, or even worse, crafting a litany of excuses. Time passes by so that we eventually find ourselves circling around the same worn path. Breaking free means breaking out of old, stale patterns, coming up against our fears, and then deciding enough is enough.

To truly break free, our commitment to our highest joy must be solid, firm, and non-negotiable—we must be *fiercely unwilling to compromise*. When we can confidently assert that we're willing to lay it all on the line for something—a creative project, business venture, or cause—that's when we know we've shifted from being a passive spectator to actively having our skin in the game.

To be an individual, to be true to yourself, to follow your own inner rhythm is the most difficult path to take, but it is the only path where you'll find true happiness and joy. Life is not about comfort or security, it is about growth and movement and sharing.

CREATIVE STORY BY ANDREA SACCONE SNYDER

"Diary log: May 27th 2012 Oahu, HI. Pinch me, I am living a dream. I don't know how I got here, but the song on my iPod at this moment, the one that has been my anthem for three months as I prepared to come on this solo trip to Hawaii is simultaneously blaring overhead in the beach side coffee shop on Oahu, where I blissfully reside for the moment.

As I sit here in complete gratitude for this experience, for all that has come before this and all that has gotten me here. I have a sketchpad, a cup of water, my watercolor pencils, and a giant chai latte. It's been three hours and it feels like ten minutes. I am in the flow. I have never been more certain of who I am, or what I need to do. I am an artist and I must create.

You see, it wasn't always this way.

I am a wife, mother, business owner, coach, friend, sister, aunt, helper—you get the picture—a "super woman." Not long ago, I came to the point in my life where things couldn't continue as they were or the system that held it all together—me—was going to break down, BURN OUT, and implode. It would not be pretty.

Fourteen years earlier, I had married David, a beautiful soul of a man—an artist, musician, and overall Renaissance man with gifts that abound, whom I met in 1989 at an art college in NY State. I was a mere nineteen years old, but I knew he was the one.

I am a hairstylist, a third-generation hairstylist, and salon owner. I did not start out to be a hairdresser, to keep the dream alive. No, I was a "real artist" and wanted to diverge from the pack to follow my dreams of living the boho life: get a loft in NYC, paint all day for high paying patrons and it galleries, while enjoying long European style dinners with a table full of laughing friends, the white twinkle lights strung overhead, giving witness to the spewing creativity that would come forth from our raucous conversations.

What really happened was that after David and I moved in together, it became frighteningly apparent that one of us needed to get a real job. School could be placed on hold, I thought. I could always do my own art on the side to satisfy my soul. I would work in my mother's salon; go to school at night to finish my degree.

I attended the local beauty school and graduated a year later. I began working in my mother's salon and started to make good money. I enjoyed the work and was really good at it. I decided to move on from my mother's small salon, to one of the high-end salons a few towns away. Dave continued to paint, show his work, do his music and hold down a not-very-high-paying day job.

At the salon I was the rock star stylist. I drifted farther and farther away from my own art. After standing on my feet in stylish and uncomfortable shoes for 10+ hours a day, I would come home and vegetate on the couch, growing angrier and angrier inside, but not yet fully understanding why.

My painting had always been a form of self-expression, one that I used to understand my inner world. My family never really understood the art thing or me. I was the weird one in a family of conventional thinkers. Dave of course got it, and me, and from day one encouraged me to get off of the couch and paint. I didn't. We fought. I ate. He painted. I cried. He left. I cried. I blamed, I ate. He came back. He painted. Dave did his best to motivate me. He loved me and saw my soul withering. I cried, I yelled. I blamed, and vegged out some more. I'd move an inch and give up. I cried on the shoulders of friends about being "a blocked artist." This went on for years. Finally, Dave and I married, moved cross-country, had a son, and opened a salon. We were happy and successful. Dave painted, wrote music, and stayed home with our son. I dabbled in art. I was still angry, but I was able to express myself enough in my work in the salon and my business, that it kept me alive.

I started meditating.

One day I realized how it was me all along. I was the one to blame. I was the one I was angry at. I was the one I had betrayed. I had given my power away. I was projecting all of my art dreams onto my husband. I let him be the artist for me. Let him carry my weight all of those years. I let him be **my voice**, while I bound my own, for almost twenty years!

Wow, what a breakthrough! I told my husband what I had discovered. He agreed. We cried, happy tears. I was exhausted, but I began the process of reclaiming my voice, my inner artist, my life, and myself. Dave encouraged me. My voice was now returning and it was joyful. This was hard work, and I desperately needed time to process, to set a vision for a future that would include my making time and space for art in my life. God, I needed a vacation.

Soon after, at the salon, through a series of synchronistic events and a creative barter with a client, I ended up on beach in Hawaii, where, essentially, everything changed.

> Fast forward to now, two years later. I've learned to take responsibility for my gift and no longer give my power away to another. I have found my voice again, and now I must paint, draw, write, whatever it is that longs to come forth. I can no longer hold on to it. I am letting go. I surrender to it, like the air that I breathe. I breathe in inspiration from everywhere, and I breathe out and let go of the breath of art. Instead of judging it harshly, I look at it with the eyes of a mother, see its worth, and give name to it. This is my practice, a process that will be my companion from now on, in gratitude to the mystery and circle of life."

Fear is what stops us from following our creative yearnings. We have responsibilities; we have duties; we have obligations. If we listen to our soul's longing for growth and creative expression, our lives, we think, will fall apart. Nothing will "get done." Perhaps, for a time things may fall a little to pieces, but a radical shift in our thinking is going to stir things up. To go from merely reacting to the circumstances of our lives to listening to the inner guidance of our soul is going to have a major impact on our lives. It won't happen overnight. It takes practice; it takes focus and discipline.

Why? There's simply too much competition for our thoughts. Unless we consciously choose to make this shift, the seductive and easy life of the familiar will lull us back into our old way of thinking. The thing to remember is that the cost of this old way of thinking is far too great and the rewards far too few.

Avoiding change takes much more energy than embracing it. Your intuition must become stronger than all other voices in your life. This is the only way to put the fear in its place.

There are no short cuts. To grow means to stretch. It means to put yourself in new and challenging situations. It means to give

of yourself in ways that you never thought possible. It means to become the person you always dreamed you could become.
You owe it to yourself to choose to be free.

Question: How can you break free?
Activity: Try one of the listed suggestions to create a shift in your creative life. It doesn't have to be life-altering, but go for something that really feels empowering and enlivening. Dazzle yourself a little. Experiment even in the smallest way. Be curious. Seek out the wonder. Lose yourself a little. Make yourself just a little bit excited. Have fun with it and let it carry your creative work into uncharted territory.
Inspiration: Virgina Satir, the pioneer of family therapy, devised **Five Freedoms** needed to become fully human. I find them highly empowering and can see the benefit in using them to call forth a more fully human creative expression from each one of us.

The Five Freedoms

1. The freedom to see and hear what is here, instead of what "should" be, was, or will be.
2. The freedom to say what you feel and think, instead of what you "should" feel and think.
3. The freedom to feel what you feel, instead of what you "ought" to feel.
4. The freedom to ask for what you want, instead of always waiting for permission.
5. The freedom to take risks on you own behalf, instead of choosing to be only "secure".

PART II

HONOR YOUR MUSE

HONOR YOUR MUSE

Often the Muse will not respond to direct and logical requests. She must be lured in with the playful and gentle.
— Jill Badonsky

The muse on my shoulder is very sensitive and does not abide claptrap of any kind... Only when I am totally immersed... absorbed in work... does she allow something magical to happen and I become aware of a faint heartbeat and gentle breath emanating from my brush. — Catherine Stock

FOR CENTURIES, ARTISTS, POETS, MUSICIANS, ACTORS, AND OTHER creative geniuses—both famous and unknown—invoked the Muse before engaging in a large creative work. This invocation was typically a plea for divine intervention and protection so that the work, in its raw and vulnerable stage, could grow and develop without interference, until it was time to be born into the world.

There is great wisdom in this practice, as we'll soon discover on our journey together. In this section, we'll take the practice even further by focusing on honoring and cultivating a sacred relationship with the Muse, which, if entered authentically, will forever change the way you relate to the creative process.

But first let's lay the foundation. Why tread so carefully? Why focus so much on cultivating a relationship with the Muse? Why does it matter?

If you've ever sat down to create, but felt no inspiration or passion with all your efforts falling flat, you've had a glimpse of the importance of getting some buy-in from your Muse. To put it bluntly, the Muse is fickle. She can show up for days gifting you with big bursts of ideas and energy, and then, without notice, she can turn her back on you leaving you feeling hurt and abandoned.

Perhaps you assume there's nothing you can do about this. I used to assume the same thing until I discovered that a good flow with the Muse wasn't random at all. It was based on my willingness to show up regularly, get out of the way and let her lead. Aha! When that light bulb went on, my creative life literally transformed overnight. Creativity is a two-way street. To get help from this wondrous source of inspiration and ideas, I had to do my part. As with any relationship, I had to get to know her—her likes and dislikes, what worked, what didn't and what she needed from me.

Besides being fickle, I discovered that the Muse is also mysterious. She cannot be pinned down, fully defined, or completely understood. If I try to grab onto her, she morphs and slips through my fingers.

She's also rather wild. It's easiest to think of her as an untamed animal—you cannot approach her too quickly, too loudly, or with too many demands. Instead, she responds best to respect, along with an open-hearted willingness to yield to her guidance.

Others have observed additional qualities about her. In a blog piece written a few years ago, writer Jonathan Zap observed that the Muse doesn't like it when we focus on certain aspects of our work or focus on them at the wrong time. Rather, she has her own ideas about what's emerging and what she wants to express. Zap suggests our creativity flows better if we yield to that. Otherwise, she might turn off that flow and abandon us for a while. Better to tune into to what Zap refers to as the "heat" around certain projects, which is essentially a green light to proceed. Without that heat, the creative process becomes a wrestling match with resistance. The Muse needs to be coddled as well as placated and nurtured—this keeps the door open to the endless abundance of ideas and output.

Though I've been writing for decades, it's only been in the past few years that I discovered how powerful it is to work with my Muse. Now, I cannot imagine approaching my creative projects any other way.

While I refer to a singular muse, as in "the Muse" or "my Muse" (capitalized out of respect), the word *muse* is usually referred to in the plural as "the Muses," which in Greek mythology are known as the nine daughters of Zeus and Mnemosyne. In Hesiod's poem, *Theogony*, the nine sisters are referred to by name: *

Erato - (Lovely), Love Poems
Euterpe - (Delightful), Flute Playing
Kalliope - (Calliope) (the Beautiful-Voiced), Epic Poetry
Kleio - (Cleio) (Celebrate), History
Melpomene - (Songstress), Tragedy
Ourania - (Urania) (Heavenly One), Astrology
Polymnia - (Polyhymnia) (Many Hymns), Sacred Music
Terpsichore - (Dance-Enjoying), Dance
Thaleia - (Blooming One), Comedy

* www.mythagora.com/bios/muses.html

This is wonderfully poetic and worthy of further investigation, but for our purposes, we'll refer to the singular Muse, since focusing on more than one Muse or Inner Voice would be too confusing.

REFLECTION QUESTION

Do you currently feel connected with your Muse? You may meditate on this today, write about it in your Creative Alchemy journal, discuss it with a friend, or all three.

BEFORE WE BEGIN

- Set an intention for this section.
- Spend time writing in your CA journal about your current relationship with your Muse.
- Open the space in your heart for your Muse.

6
UNLEARNING

We must be willing to sit on the edge of mystery and unlearn what has helped guide us in the past but is no longer useful. — Robert Wicks

The most useful piece of learning for the uses of life is to unlearn what is untrue. — Antisthenes

TO OPEN A CONNECTION WITH THE MUSE, WE FIRST NEED TO EMPTY ourselves to create space for the new. I don't mean physical space; I mean the space inside of our heads that is cluttered with a whole bunch of negative advice, opinions, feedback, and criticism. Inherited from parents, teachers, neighbors, friends, extended family, etc., these nasty gremlins (as some people like to call them) can derail even the most amazing and exciting project.

They need to go! They're stowaways that have moved in, becoming permanent residents. It's time to kick them out! Their distractions, crazy-making, and sabotage are taking up much-needed real estate, and it's high time we claim that space for what we want. The following story from the book, *101 Zen Stories*, by Nyogen Senzaki illustrates the idea perfectly.

> *Nan-in, a Japanese master during the Meiji era (1868-1912), received a university professor who came to inquire about Zen. Rather than listen to what the Japanese master had to say, the university professor immediately began dominating the discussion with his own ideas, viewpoints, and knowledge.*
>
> *While the university professor continued to talk, Nan-in listened patiently and began preparing tea. He poured his visitor's cup full, and then kept on pouring.*
>
> *The professor watched the overflow until he no longer could restrain himself. "Stop!" he said. "The cup is overfull. No more will go in!"*
>
> *"Yes," Nan-in said. "And like this cup, you too are overfilled with your own opinions and speculations. How can I show you Zen unless you first empty your cup?"*

A question arises: How will you know what to let go? In a cluttered room, it's difficult to see what's worth keeping and what must go. First, you might take stock of what's there. Then ask yourself, "Which of these things will help me lead a healthy balanced life?" "Which of these things will hold me back?" As applied to creativity, you can substitute "ideas, beliefs, expectations, assumptions" in place of "things."

My biggest creative obstacles were:

1. *There isn't enough time.* With working, kids, household stuff, who has time to sit down and really dedicate oneself to large creative projects?
2. *What I want to write doesn't matter.* I truly believed that no one wanted to read what I had to say.
3. *What I want to write has been said before.* I often became

overwhelmed by the sheer number of books in the world and didn't believe there was room for mine.
4. *I'm not good enough.* This belief crippled me more than all the others combined because I truly felt that I didn't have enough raw talent to allow me to be heard in a world of other, far more talented writers.

Perhaps you can relate. Take a moment now and tune in to see if you can catch a glimpse of one of these sneaky beliefs running like a ticker tape through your life. Don't judge or criticize yourself. Just notice and observe. Awareness is the first step in creating space in your creative life.

Now, take a couple of minutes and reflect on the statement below. Tape it on your bathroom mirror, refrigerator, or computer screen so you won't forget it.

Closing old doors is a signal to the universe that I'm ready to open new ones.

When you're willing to let go of old things, you become a magnet for new opportunities. How do I know? I've witnessed it dozens of times in my own life and in the lives of others. The only way you'll know for sure is to try it for yourself.

As children, most of us engaged in many creative games, using our imaginations, pretending and making things out of whatever we had available. Unfortunately, once we're in school, these free-spirited games become more limited, leaving our creative expression to become more controlled and contrived.

What's needed here is to become more child-like—open and receptive to the inner whispers, the flow of ideas that want to spring forth unimpeded. To do that we need to become aware of what's taking up space and blocking the flow. Let's look at some common areas that can sabotage our creative process:

FEAR AND PERFECTIONISM

As Sir Ken Robinson says in his TedTalk about education and creativity, "If you're not prepared to do something wrong, you'll never come up with anything original." It's our fear of failure that burdens our creative expression. This clearly needs to be unlearned. Often, it's a teacher's harsh critique, a parent's unkind words, or our peers' teasing that causes feelings of inadequacy, thus leading us to restrict our creative output.

COMPARING

Comparing our work with others can lead to the misperception that we're not good enough. We give up before we even find our voice or our footing in the creative world. Everything takes practice and time. Very few of us are born child prodigies with talent oozing from our pores. Instead, what we have are gifts that can be cultivated and refined over time. Comparing others' outsides with our insides also stops us in our tracks. We can get caught up imagining that others have it easier due to some extra talent, resources, luck, support, etc., that we feel is sorely lacking in our lives.

BAD HABITS

As we prioritize making a living, family and social obligations, upkeep of our home, physical exercise, etc., we often back-burner our creativity until it feels distant and remote. We get used to living without it. We justify it by saying we don't have enough time, but inside there is a longing to reconnect with that part of ourselves. Perhaps there is a project idea that comes to us, causing us to wonder how in the world we'll ever find a way to make it happen. Sometimes, even when we have the time, we find ourselves doing anything but our cherished creative work.

FEELING UNWORTHY AND UNAPPRECIATED

We may believe that we don't have what it takes, or even if we did, no one would care. We've lost touch with the joy of being creative just for the sake of doing it. We're stopping ourselves because we're too intimidated to really own being a writer or painter or photographer.

When I ran my first writer's group for women, many of the members were afraid to call themselves writers because they hadn't published. Before they shared their work, most of them apologized for it, stating that it probably wasn't very good. First, I told them that they never needed to apologize again for expressing themselves, and then I said if they loved writing and wrote regularly, they were writers. While being published is a wonderful result of one's diligence and work as writer, it isn't what makes someone a writer.

THE IMPORTANCE OF SPACIOUSNESS

When it comes to creativity, spaciousness is SO important, both within as well as without—the space between words, the gaps between actions, the empty container, the void of possibility from which all creative acts arise.

Slowing down and creating space is a necessary part of laying the foundation for a strong relationship with one's Muse. Most of us have lives crammed not only with the internal stuff listed above, but also lives filled with busyness. We're out of breath, running around putting out fires, making it nearly impossible to hear the subtle whispers of our Muse.

Question: What do you need to unlearn to make space for creativity and the whispers of the Muse in your life?
Activity: Take one of your mason jars—decorate it if you like—and label it RELEASE. Cut up some small slips of paper that you can easily write on and fold up into small pieces. Every time you notice a bad habit or behavior, a negative thought or criticism, a fear of failure or worry about not being good enough, write it down, and then release it into the jar to make space for your Muse. Trust me, you're Muse will thank you. There isn't enough room for these negative gremlins and your Muse in one space.
Inspiration: Watch the Ira Glass video "The Gap," on Vimeo or YouTube.

7
TUNING IN

So cheat your landlord if you can and must, but do not try to shortchange the Muse. It cannot be done. You can't fake quality any more than you can fake a good meal. — William S. Burroughs

This is the other secret that real artists know and wannabe writers don't. When we sit down each day and do our work, power concentrates around us. The Muse takes note of our dedication. She approves. We have earned favor in her sight. When we sit down and work, we become like a magnetized rod that attracts iron filings. Ideas come. Insights accrete. — Steven Pressfield

AS WITH ALL NEW RELATIONSHIPS, YOUR RELATIONSHIP WITH YOUR Muse must begin with courting—listening and tuning in. So many creative people I know talk about the effort, struggle, and work needed to write, paint, act, film, sing, etc. This used to be my experience as well until I discovered *a different approach*.

Before that, I had so many ideas, needs, agendas, and pressure surrounding my writing. I was submitting my stories and essays, collecting rejection slips and occasionally getting my work out there. But it was a haphazard approach so jacked up with pressure that it drained the joy out of the process. Writing became work and ceased to be fun.

This all changed when I learned to work with my Muse *on her terms* and not expect her to perform to my expectations. This doesn't mean, as some people suspect, that we need to wait until the mood strikes or until we feel overcome with inspiration. Not at all. What it does mean is that *we need to follow the Muse where she wants to go.*

And we need to show up. A lot.

To get to know this mysterious, creative energy behind our ideas and passion, it's important to connect regularly with your Muse —to adore, cherish and, by all means, celebrate her. In fact, if you treat her with the utmost respect, consistently tuning into her needs, she will bless you with incredible gifts. If, however, you neglect her for long stretches of time, and then sit down and expect her to do your bidding, she'll refuse to cooperate, leaving you empty-handed when you need her most.

As I mentioned earlier, it's a two-way street of give and take. For example, you may want to finish that novel, painting, or song, but your Muse may want you to start something completely new. Or you may want to start something new, but your Muse wants to revise that play or work in a completely different medium. Regardless of what your Muse wants, I've found the best approach is to work on whatever you feel intuitively nudged to do. In fact, *an intuitive nudge is one of the ways your Muse communicates with you.* Another way is by sending you an inspiration to do something seemingly out of nowhere, usually in the most unlikely places: while driving, while vacuuming, in the shower, in our dreams, etc. Think of it as the spark needed to light the fire.

When that spark does come, grab onto it, hold it close to your heart, and respond as quickly as possible by doing something with that spark. At the very least write it down and tuck it away for safekeeping. If you just ignore it while going about the business of your life, your Muse will see you rejecting her, so that when you finally do have time for her, she may not be available.

One way I've found to keep my Muse happy has been to establish a daily writing practice so that no matter what else is happening in my life, I'm committed to showing up and spending time with her. I write around 1,000 words (some days more and some days less). This has worked wonders. Plus, it sets a creative tone to the day. Of course, there are times when life pulls me away and I miss my morning writing, but it is such a foundational piece of my life that I find I can easily return to it.

Cultivating a relationship with your Muse is a dance. It's a relationship. It's a collaboration. And one that demands the utmost respect.

SOME QUALITIES OF THE MUSE

- Spontaneous
- Fluid and flexible
- Feeling-based and irrational
- In the moment
- Dream-like, ethereal
- Gift giver
- Subtle
- Communicates in whispers and nudges

HOW TO CONNECT

- Tune in
- Notice
- Listen
- Acknowledge
- Take action
- Appreciate
- Repeat

It's that simple. We'll expand on ways to make friends and deepen the relationship in the next chapter.

Question: What does your Muse want from you right now?
Activity: Write a letter to your Muse in your CA journal. Introduce yourself and share whatever's in your heart. Then listen and see if she responds.
Inspiration: Read *The Invitation* by Oriah Mountain Dreamer.

8
MAKING FRIENDS

The muse whispers to you when she chooses and you can't tell her to come back later because you quickly learn in this business that she might not come back at all. — Terry Brooks

I just really allowed my muse to be my guide and I just go with whatever I'm feeling. — K.D. Lang

MAKING FRIENDS WITH YOUR MUSE IS A LIFELONG ADVENTURE. THIS creative partnership is a unique and rewarding relationship that can be cultivated in many ways. Ideally, you'll want to experiment to see what truly resonates. There's no right or wrong way to keep the energy enlivened in this relationship; however, I will say that trust is an essential ingredient.

Your friends don't like to be ignored—the same holds true for your Muse. When life is full, excuses come way too easily and your creative life moves down your priority list or gets turned off altogether. The connection to your Muse grows cold, so much so, that it can feel daunting to reconnect. Just as our muscles atrophy after a long time away from the gym, our creative muscles also atrophy and need time, plus practice, to warm up again.

Lucky for us, it can be fun courting one's Muse. There are so many ways to entice her to play: music, essential oils, going on a creative date, setting up a sacred space, working with a creative buddy, journaling, taking a course, etc. The point is to just begin. Don't be shy. Take a step. Make a gesture. Show up. These simple steps go a long way when it comes to making friends with your Muse.

She'll respond. If not right away, eventually you will feel her nudges and hear her whispers. She may wake you up in the middle of the night with an image, phrase or an entire idea. She may speak to you through the words of a song, a roadside sign, a passage in a book, etc. She may send you a powerful dream or touch you through a mystical poem. Her language is broad and deep as well as unpredictable. The trick is to sense her, recognize when she's around. As we all do, **she loves to be noticed and adored**. When she does offer you gifts, by all means thank her! Gratitude fans the flames of this love affair, keeping the fire burning bright, warming the coals with the heat of inspiration just when you need it.

CREATIVE STORY BY SHARI DANIELS

> "Before readying myself to pen this page, I light a candle or two, set my Pandora station to David Nevue and lay my hands upon the hand-stitched quilt draped across my writing table. As my fingertips graze over the intricate stitches put there by me so many years before, I slow down to breathe in this sacred container of space. My Artist Warrior stands within eyesight to remind me not to be afraid. Fresh acorns adorn a clay heart; symbols of starting small and having faith it will

grow to something more and of course, a reminder to write from my heart.

"I'm here, Gabby. Ready, in heart, mind, body and spirit," I breathe out. "Please be here to inspire me. Give me the words I need to be said to the world today. Help me say them with love."

Some people call this "guide" a muse, their creativity, soul, spirit or God. Whatever the title, it doesn't matter, but I believe mine is Archangel Gabriel, the angel of communication, a messenger from God. For short, I call her Gabby. And she is quite pleased that I'm writing about her today.

I didn't always know I had an angel to guide me in my writing. In fact, for years, my writing was just whiny girl writing that my victimized mind liked to tell stories of. Julie Cameron, in the Artist's Way, wrote, "We are victims of our own internalized perfectionist, a nasty internal critic, the Censor, who resides in our left brain and keeps up a constant stream of subversive remarks that are often disguised as the truth." I named this voice Bernice. Now I can easily recognize her when she shows up. If I don't, my writing will dwell in this darkness for pages and pages. I then call upon Gabby to save me and take me to the other side.

Gabby not only helps me in the physical act of writing, but she also can magically make sure I pull out just the right book for the words I need, or will jaunt the memory of my past to match up to what I am thinking of, or she'll even send me the people I need, and the best? Mail.

This morning, when I called upon her, I began my writing already blocked. I wanted the perfect lead for this piece and I didn't have it. I was sure there was one lost away in my notebooks, but who has time to go digging? So, I just sat there, waiting impatiently, listening to Bernice condemn me for my lack of organization. Pretty soon, I heard her voice.

"For Pete's Sake, Shari, are you going to claim writer's block because of this? You know that to draft, you start with anything, write garbage, open a vein, just get it all out on the page. You can't fret over a lead if you don't have a darn thing on the page. You know this already. Now giddy-up."

"Geez, yes. I do know this. Thank you for the kick in the pants, Gabby, and hello. You are a little pushy today," I told her.

"There's no time for coddling today, let's get something finished," she pushes on.

The mail carrier knocked on my door. She only does this with packages. I was excited as I knew there would be something I need for my writing piece. I was not disappointed. An Uppercase magazine with the front cover message across the page screaming, "You Have Exactly What It Takes" and a special Brave Girls' Club package loaded with "Be Your Own Hero" reminders.

"Thank you, Gabby," I whispered. My heart warmed.

Back at my notebook, I had a renewed sense of empowerment. I followed Gabby's instructions and let-er-rip. More words came out than were necessary, but they came. My hand refused to stop. Bliss is this sweet savory place of writing in flow with a loss of time, place and even missing a meal.

Yes, this is how it goes. . . when I write with Gabby."

In his book, *Daily Rituals: How Artists Work*, Mason Curry shares the daily routine and habits of 161 novelists, poets, playwrights, painters, philosophers, scientists, mathematicians, etc. What's surprising to discover is that most didn't have ideal circumstances in which to create, but instead found ways to express themselves despite those circumstances. One arose extra early, while another stayed up late. One took long daily walks, while another indulged in large quantities of coffee. One ate the same food every day, while another spent the morning naked. One writer I know always wears a certain hat when she's working on a book.

When I was younger, I used to be a night owl and did my best creative work late at night. As I moved into mid-life, my entire sleeping patterns shifted. Now I love getting up early—my energy is super charged and I get loads accomplished. This carries me throughout the entire day. Then just after dinner, I begin to wind down and look forward to getting to sleep, usually between nine and ten. I could never have imagined myself living this way, but it's what my body seems to need, so I comply, and it works.

The point is to find your rhythm—what works for you—trust it and stick with it. You can experiment with your own daily routine. Below is a list of suggestions to help you befriend your Muse. We'll be exploring some of these in-depth throughout the book; the others are self-explanatory.

7 WAYS TO BEFRIEND YOUR MUSE

1. Follow a daily creative ritual
2. Keep a dream journal
3. Go on regular creative dates
4. Create a sacred space
5. Spend time in meditation and prayer
6. Write to her in your journal
7. Spend time in nature

Regardless of what you choose, have fun with it! Creativity is play, after all. One clear sign that you aren't working with your Muse is that you're struggling and your creative time feels like work. With the Muse, it mostly feels effortless, magical, and even transcendent because when it's flowing time and space seem to disappear. This is why it's SO important to connect with your Muse: it's where the joy lives!

∾

Question: What do you need for your Muse to thrive?

Activity: Create a simple ritual or write a prayer that puts you in the mood to create.

Inspiration: *Steal Like an Artist: 10 Things Nobody Told You About Being Creative* by Austin Kleon.

9
CARING AND FEEDING

Laughing in my ear is a muse amused by how I paint her whims on paper with silly words. — Richelle Goodrich

The muse on my shoulder is very sensitive and does not abide claptrap of any kind... Only when I am totally immersed... absorbed in work... does she allow something magical to happen and I become aware of a faint heartbeat and gentle breath emanating from my brush. — Catherine Stock

MANY OF US WAIT TO BE INSPIRED BEFORE WE SIT DOWN TO CREATE. Sound familiar? Maybe you're waiting for things to settle down a bit, or to become more of an expert, or for your idea to gel a little more. Unfortunately, this approach takes away from the regular practice necessary to build a strong relationship with your Muse.

Moving between your everyday ordinary world and the deep inner world of your imagination takes practice. Many talented artists have been carried away by these inner worlds unable to anchor themselves in the mundane day-to-day world. Others hold back from these inner worlds preferring safety and dry land, but end up feeling frustrated from either not producing much or producing mediocre work.

Thus, cultivating a strong relationship with your Muse is an essential ingredient of the creative process. After years of personal struggle with my own writing, I now consider it essential to the creative process. In other words, I cannot imagine doing it any other way.

Let's explore some specific ways to honor the Muse more in depth:

WILLINGNESS

Willingness is a great first step in surrendering to the larger creative realm of the unseen. Willingness means you're ready to receive, you're ready to do your part in the creative partnership, and you're ready to witness the magic of the formless coming into form. Recognizing your role as midwife to this realm, you can thus demonstrate your humility, respect, and love, opening many doors to greater wisdom and inspiration.

In addition, there's nothing worse than "trying" to create something. It's all struggle and effort, and not at all fulfilling. Why? For one thing, you're usually going at it alone, rather than partnering with the Muse.

With the Muse, there's no trying, only allowing.

INTENTION

Setting an intention allows you to envision where you'd like to go. The wind then carries you on your journey into the unknown, its breath infusing you with the energy to manifest, its joy fueling your movement forward regardless of the obstacles in your path. Intention is your inner radiance expressed through your actions. Each step uses that intention to create alchemy—the transformational process, which transports our ideas from the unseen realm into the realm of time and space where they can be seen and experienced.

SHOWING UP

In her fabulous book, *Daring Greatly*, author Brené Brown writes, "The willingness to show up changes us. It makes us a little braver each time." She's right. It does change us, especially when we realize that no one can do it for us. We must hold the brush in our hand, pick up the instrument, put our rear end in the chair, take the camera out of the bag, memorize our lines, put on our dance clothes, etc. Each time we do, it builds our courage and our confidence. It's the well-known 10,000 hours of practice that makes us good at something. Sure, there are the uber-talented who are born miles ahead of us. But some of them don't ever do anything with those gifts, or they take them for granted, or they crash and burn early on in their creative careers. No one can rely on talent alone. You still must show up regularly to do anything worthwhile.

LISTENING

The Muse often speaks in whispers so you need to be very quiet to hear her. It requires really tuning in and listening to her nudges, clues, hints, synchronicities, dreams, visions, fragments of ideas, and so on. It's imperative that you capture these creative bits and pieces as they float through your consciousness because you never know where one of them might lead.

GETTING OUT OF THE WAY

Working with the Muse means getting your identity and personality out of the way, which is another way of saying keeping your ego in check. Wanting the identity of a writer or artist or even worse, creating art only because you want to be rich and famous blocks the flow. If you're focused too much on the result and creating only because you want to feel better about yourself, you're going to have a hard time sustaining your connection with the Muse. Far better to enter the creative process because you love every blessed moment of it, meaning you'd do it whether or not you're ever recognized or paid for it.

Of course, this doesn't mean you don't deserve to be recognized or paid, only that it probably shouldn't be the main reason you're making art. Ideally, creativity ought to be a mad love affair with your Muse, with the reward being some beautiful, original creations you want to share with the world. If you make money and become famous after that, GREAT! In the meantime, just show up and allow what wants to come through you, come through. It's that simple. You're a uniquely-tuned instrument allowing Life to play through you. From this viewpoint, art is a wondrous co-creation, which releases the strain and struggle so that it becomes a sacred dance of celebration and joy.

I invite you with love to take a refreshing, deep breath and really take this all in. Your Muse is counting on you to respond to her offerings. The more you're willing to receive, the more she'll offer up. If you aren't willing to do anything with her gifts, she'll probably stop offering them. She may even go silent, leaving you to struggle on your own for a while until she senses you appreciate her again. I know firsthand how awful that can be! Once you taste the sweet nectar of working in sync with your Muse, you'll never, ever want to work alone again. Do your best to keep her happy and she'll be there waiting for you in the wings at your beck and call!

Question: How do you honor your Muse?
Activity: Schedule some time with your Muse at least once a week (or more). Look at your calendar and see where you can find space during the next five weeks to show up for your Muse. It can be 20-minute blocks of time, an hour, three hours, or a mix. If you haven't been keeping a regular creative schedule, start with baby steps. If you have, perhaps you'd like to deepen your connection with your Muse. Whatever you'd like to focus on, make that part of your sacred creative practice.
Inspiration: Read *Bird by Bird* by Anne Lamott.

10
PRIORITIES AND BOUNDARIES

Things which matter most must never be at the mercy of things which matter least. — Johann Wolfgang von Goethe

Daring to set boundaries is about having the courage to love ourselves, even when we risk disappointing others. — Brené Brown

PRIORITIES AND BOUNDARIES ARE TWO POWERFUL ALLIES, THAT WHEN teamed up, allow the creative flow to move forward unimpeded. First, you clear the space by making your creative time an important part of your overall schedule. Then, once the space is cleared, you protect it by putting a strong, healthy fence around it.

PRIORITIES

At the end of the day, how often do you wonder where the time went? How about at the end of a week, a month, or even a year?

Do you also question what you accomplished during that time? Do you ever have a sense that time got away from you? That the minutes, hours, and days whizzed past you like a runaway train before you even realized you were being left behind?

No major creative projects happen overnight, nor do they happen without planning. Creative people typically don't look like the most organized people on the planet, and yet many of them manage to produce a solid body of work. How? They put it high up on their list of priorities. Nothing less will do than *making time* to do creative work.

Your Muse must be important enough to make time for her. She thrives on attention and support; she withers with neglect.

Talent is not enough. Skills are not enough. Passion is not enough. All are necessary but what really changes the game, what really drives the ball home are regular, consistent commitments of time. This is what wins the Muse over to your cause. This is what opens the flow for the good stuff to appear. This is what facilitates a powerful mix of all those other ingredients.

It took me years of struggling to really grasp how I was getting in my own way. I fantasized about some magical time in the future when my life would be easier and I would have plenty of time to write. But life doesn't work that way. It has this annoying way of throwing obstacles, distractions, and too much stuff to do in our paths, giving us endless reasons not to create. And we fall for it! We busy ourselves with all sorts of time-wasting, energy-sucking things when if we really stopped for a second and got honest with ourselves, we'd see that time is not the enemy—we are! It all boils down to this:

. . .

If it's important enough to me, I'll show up. If not, I won't.

If your creativity isn't close to the top of your list most of the time, it probably doesn't make sense to keep talking about how much you long to do something creative. Action is what inspires your Muse to partner with you. Nothing less will do.

BOUNDARIES

Once you've made the commitment and carved out the time, then you'll need to protect it. Think of wolves at the door trying to get to your innocent little lamb, wanting to tear her limb from limb. What can you do to protect her?

Boundaries strengthen your creative life by putting a protective border around your time and space so that your Muse can show up without risk of interruption and interference. Good, clear communication makes this possible. Scheduling creative time comes first, followed by letting the people in your life know what you're up to.

HERE ARE SOME RECOMMENDED STEPS

1. Go into your sacred space
2. Tune out the world and tune into your Muse
3. Breathe
4. Warm up by doing some simple exercises in your chosen creative medium
5. Stick to your time or extend if you wish
6. Let go of the creative realm
7. Re-enter the world

Interruptions will inevitably happen, and when they do, meet them with love and kindness. Speak your truth about what you're doing and what you need in a clear, simple way. Offer to connect when you're finished (or another time). Tell the interrupter you'll respond to their needs at that time.

Setting healthy, loving boundaries teaches the people in your life how to treat you. You're simply asking for respect. Once they learn that you're deeply committed to honoring your creative time, they'll hold it with the same respect you do.

It's important not to react in a negative way. Yes, it's frustrating to have the creative flow interrupted and get knocked out of the zone; however, it will do no good to handle it badly. You'll be far better off stating your needs clearly in a neutral tone so that you can maintain your creative equilibrium.

Putting yourself within a boundary-protected sanctuary grants you permission to create freely, without hindrance or pressure during the time you scheduled for yourself. Weak boundaries cause many creative people to fall short of their creative goals and aspirations. Learning to fiercely protect your creative time will go a long way in helping ward off the ever-present distractions and the magnetic pull of resistance that draws you away from your Muse.

Honoring your Muse is an evolving journey that asks a lot, but gives a whole lot in return. You're essentially paying it forward with her. Why? Because in exchange for your commitment and loyalty, she will pay you constant, often mind-blowing dividends that will make your jaws drop in awe at the gifts she's willing to give *to and through* you. As you cultivate this partnership, all the agonizing and creative struggles will evaporate. What remains will be pure creative output.

∽

Question: Where are you right now with prioritizing your creative time and setting loving boundaries around it?

Activity: If you're in a good place with priorities and boundaries, practice strengthening them. If you're not, start by observing yourself for several days and notice when you compromise your own needs, when you say yes, when you want to say no, and when you let others override your boundaries. Then practice speaking your truth, saying no when you want to say yes and fortifying your boundaries. Pay particular attention to the times when you conspire with others to sabotage yourself and your creative time. Write about your experience with priorities and boundaries in your CA journal.

Inspiration of the Day: Read *Do the Work* by Steven Pressfield.

PART III

LIGHT THE CREATIVE FIRE

LIGHT THE CREATIVE FIRE

Nobody cares if you can't dance well. Just get up and dance. Great dancers are not great because of their technique, they are great because of their passion. — Martha Graham

The soul should always stand ajar. Ready to welcome the ecstatic experience. — Emily Dickinson

IN THIS SECTION, WE'LL DIVE DEEPER INTO THE CREATIVE REALM BY examining some of the essential ingredients: imagination, tools, space, and practice. The creative process is both exhilarating and excruciating. It seduces us while it draws us in, but then occasionally leaves us frustrated or heart-broken when we can't meet our own ideals. This can cause us to sabotage and abandon our projects because we simply don't know how to bring the fullness of our vision into fruition.

In his book, *Stoking the Creative Fires: 9 Ways to Rekindle Passion and Imagination*, Phil Cousineau suggests that one way to rekindle your creative fire is to "follow the thread back to your original fire." In other words, become childlike again, look at the world with wonder, see the world with a beginner's mind, stay open and receptive the way you were when you first picked up an instrument, a paintbrush, a pencil, a script, a camera, etc. Go back to that first spark that inspired you to enter the sacred realm of the imagination, then bring the ideas you discovered there into the world of form.

This return to wonder is a fantastic first step. The trick is to have enough good chemistry with a project so that it can ignite the energy to move forward, and return to it again and again. When there is energy, curiosity, excitement, passion, love, inspiration, and joy connected with a project, it gives off heat with the motivation arising from the heart, not just the intellect.

Several years ago, I lost momentum on a memoir I was writing about my relationship with my father when a writer friend from Turkey suggested I turn it into a screenplay. Voila! The passion returned. The challenge of working in an entirely different format infused the whole project with new passion. Add to that the purchase of a laptop and a decision to write it in a café, and it all felt brand new and highly compelling.

Other times we start down the road with a project (because someone suggests it or its trendy), but it's just not a good fit. It might be easy enough to initiate it and perhaps after that initial prompting you decide to do it because 1) it might make you money; 2) people will be impressed; or 3) it's something you think you *should do*. However, as I mentioned in an earlier chapter, projects done for ego strokes, outside approval or money alone, are difficult to sustain because they're missing the childlike wonder which make creativity such a joy.

What this means is this: to truly feed your soul, the creative fire must be lit from within and come from a deep soul-resonating, intuitive place inside you. You may call this your Higher Self, if you like. This deep well within is where your authentic, original Voice lives (more on that later).

We've all had that experience in which we've read a book,

listened to a song, watched a movie and felt a bit empty afterwards. This is because it was created by the small self or intellect, which draws heavily from the hive consciousness surrounding us. Art, music, books and such that come from this place feel as though they're rehashed versions of what's gone before—they are missing the deep essence and timeless roots of a work of genius that speaks to multiple generations.

The creative work that truly feeds the soul is untainted by the outside world. Staying true to that requires nothing less than ignoring the opinions of others and trusting the ideas that want to be expressed through our unique instrument.

If you feel as though your flames are low or your fire has gone out, check in with yourself to *see if you're creating art that nourishes you at a soul level*. If not, then it's time to do some reflecting so you can free yourself from the frustrations of projects that aren't flowing. If you are, but still feel blocked, then perhaps there are other things in the way (fear of failure, perhaps) and you'll need to do what you can to coax your Muse out of hiding.

In the meantime, here are some fun ways to relight the creative flame:

- Surround yourself with creative people you admire (either in person in a group or by reading creative autobiographies)
- Attending creative events such as open mics, museums, gallery open houses, bookstores, etc.
- Take classes
- Working one-on-one with a creative coach.

Some other steps that can also get those flames roaring:

- Journal and ask the Muse what she needs.
- Test the temperature of your creative projects and

work on the ones that are warm. Put the cold ones aside for now.
- Collaborate with a partner to help you show up and hold you accountable.
- Book a retreat and shut out the world for several days.

REFLECTION QUESTION

How can you light the fire of creativity in your own life?

BEFORE WE BEGIN

- Set an intention for this section.
- Take steps to stoke the fire of creativity in your life, using the suggestions above.
- Share your experience with a creative friend.

11
THE POWER OF IMAGINATION

I am enough of an artist to draw freely upon my imagination. Imagination is more important than knowledge. Knowledge is limited. Imagination encircles the world.— Albert Einstein

Our imagination flies — we are its shadow on the earth. — Vladimir Nabokov

ALL CREATIVE IDEAS START IN OUR IMAGINATION. IT'S WHAT WE DO with those ideas that becomes art. Some ideas are difficult to translate, creating a gap between our vision and what we're able to bring forth. A powerful idea can become something entirely different once we start working with it.

Children are closer to their imaginations and sadly, the older they get, the more that connection fades. Cultivation is key. To be able to access it, we must pay attention to it. Our culture doesn't value daydreaming, however, sometimes that's exactly what's needed: a free-flowing stream of consciousness in the form of images, ideas, words, fragments of scenes, visions, etc.

The more relaxed we are about letting things flow, the more the creative juices will pour forth in abundance. Unfortunately, most of us were taught to rein all that in, to create—on demand—inside of appropriate boxes. Imagination, specifically the realm of the Muse, is messy, untamed, raw, vivid, and all over the place. It certainly doesn't fit neatly into boxes. Perhaps that's why it can be so intimidating to enter this world—it doesn't always relate well with our day-to-day responsibilities and household tasks. In fact, the two sometimes feel like polar opposites.

CREATIVE STORY BY SANDY KING

"My imagination goes with me everywhere. In fact, I never leave home without it. This a story about imagination, or more so, maybe this is the story of a mouse.

As a child, I was told that I had a vivid imagination. I still use that vivid imagination in my creative life, but have only recently been aware of its power. To use it, run with it, let it take me where it wants.

I started playing with watercolours about a few years ago with the intention of enjoying their unique quality in the pages of my art. In the process of learning how to combine 'wet on wet' pigment, and 'lifting' color to create depth in the image using a dry brush, a mouse I would come to call Wiston seemed to be art-bombing my artwork. I would have said he came out of nowhere. He wasn't a new character in the world, of course.

Even as my mouse was surfacing in the world of my art, the process of becoming the artist that I am today was a blending of all the concepts I was being exposed to through the alchemy of creativity.

Through the quiet times, I set aside time to really listen to my imagination and pay attention to the 'signs and messages' that were everywhere.

But more than listening to it run in the background like I'd been doing in the past, I created windows of opportunity to truly listen, with pen at the ready, and I started documenting its playful script.

When I sit with my sketchbook, it's my imagination that comes through the pencil of Wiston (my new-found friend) living his life from what I imagine him to be doing or feeling.

I created a 3D version of the watercolor naked mouse to accompany me on my travels; it was my imagination at work doing what it wanted to do. What will happen if I lift this character off the page and made him into a tangible being? What will he wear? Where he will want to go and what will he want to see when he gets there? The possibilities are endless. Just imagine.

And so began the story of Wiston the Mouse."

BUILD A BRIDGE

What to do? Build a supportive bridge between imagination and everyday life. Be easy on yourself. Recognize that these two worlds are quite different from each other and take your time transitioning between them. When you shift too abruptly from one to another, it can be jarring for you as well as the people around you. When you're hanging out in the creative zone, time disappears. This can wreak havoc on other people in your life. It helps to set a timer so that you have time to decompress before your duties call you back from the land of imagination.

Think of your imagination as a destination, a far-off land you go to explore and get inspired, a retreat from the ordinary and the mundane. When you head off into this special place, see it as an adventure, a place that holds secrets and mysteries that are waiting for you to discover and share them with words, colors, sound, texture, action, etc. You are the interpreter of this holy realm. Only you know how to excavate just the right pieces of the puzzle to create something that will uplift, move, and touch others.

I recommend you travel light for this adventure so that you can stay receptive. No plans are needed, only an opening of all your senses, including your intuition—the part of you that feels and knows things that cannot be seen. Deep listening and observing allow for a wonderful flow of ideas to pour forth. All you need to do is allow yourself to tune in and receive from this infinite well of creation. You become the receiver. With these gifts, you create and shift into the role of giver, while others become the receiver of your creation, completing the sacred circle of life.

Once you learn to move into it fluidly, you'll discover just how powerful the imagination can be! Everything that exists first existed as an idea before it manifested in the physical world. Every act of creation is an act of alchemy, both within and without. Harnessing the power of imagination gives you an opportunity to consciously own and embrace your unique creative gifts and helps you tune into the ways Life wants to express itself through you.

This is a magical way to live in that it allows you to feel part of the dance of life, part of creation itself. The only thing required is for you to take the imaginative fuel you're given, utilizing it to direct your actions, and even your very service to the world around us.

You've been given the chance to be gods and goddesses (Creators) of your own mini world. How awesome is that? Have fun with it! Your responsibilities will still be there when you return.

WAYS TO SPARK THE IMAGINATION

1. Browse through photos
2. Listen to music

3. Relax and let the mind wander
4. Use writing prompts
5. Write down ideas that appear out of nowhere in your CA journal
6. Immerse yourself in other people's creativity through open mics, shows, galleries, bookstores, etc.
7. Attend a creative retreat or sign up for a course

Question: How does the transformative power of imagination touch your life and deeply impact your choices and your life path?

Activity: Take another jar. Decorate it if you like and label it CREATE. Take some small strips of paper that can easily be folded and every time your imagination sends you an idea, write it on a slip of paper, and put it into the jar.

Inspiration: Watch "29 Ways to Stay Creative" on Vimeo.

12
CREATIVE JUICE

Energy is the essence of life. Every day you decide how you're going to use it by knowing what you want and what it takes to reach that goal, and by maintaining focus. — Oprah Winfrey

The more you lose yourself in something bigger than yourself, the more energy you will have. — Norman Vincent Peale

WHERE DOES CREATIVE ENERGY COME FROM AND HOW CAN WE TAP into it? Some say creative energy and sexual energy are closely linked. While this is a bit of an oversimplification, it points to a powerhouse of resources that we draw from every day: our life force. This energy—when directed—can accomplish extraordinary things, including (through the sexual act) creating another human being.

How can we access this juice? There are a variety of ways, however for our purposes, we'll simplify it into four main sources:

1. **Emotional.** Some artists are compelled to express deep, painful feelings through their art. The energy they're drawing from is emotional.
2. **Intellectual.** Others draw from the realm of intellectual ideas, often inspired by the question, "What if?" Daydreaming and imagining different scenarios playing out sparks the fire here.
3. **Spiritual.** Sometimes energy can be extracted from our quest for meaning and purpose. This allows us to infuse it with the larger, more universal essence of life.
4. **Physical.** Some forms of art are deeply entwined with the physical, such as music, dance, and some aspects of theater. Movement triggers the flood of energy to rush forth.

Sometimes we'll draw from one source while at other times we'll draw from a combination of two or more sources that merge and power up the engine of creativity. Much depends on the project, our circumstances, and our mood.

LIMITED OR UNLIMITED?

Some scientists argue that we each have a limited allotment of energy available to us each day. Perhaps that's true, however, I suspect there's also a way to tap into a universal source of energy that is unlimited. It no longer belongs to us, but to the larger universal collective. Working with the Muse seems to dial us into this infinite source of creative juice as witnessed in the prolific work of many artists who seem to accomplish more than humanly possible.

Creative juice can arise naturally or we can go looking for it. Most of us know what gets those juices flowing, but it's always worthwhile to try something new. One fun way to get inspired is to try your hand at a completely new form of creative expression. If you're a writer, try improv or dance. If you're a dancer, try painting or photography. If you're a photographer, try singing or poetry. Perhaps you already work in multiple mediums. Then just do something, anything to stir things up. See what makes you a little afraid and take a leap out of your comfort zone. These activities can zap you into a more wakeful state and get the juices flowing.

Another tip is to take your chosen creative form, but do it in a way that pushes you to the edges of your usual territory. Switch genres. Use different tools. If you've been hanging out solo, join a group, take a class or initiate a project that requires collaboration. If you're used to working in a studio, switch to working outside in nature. Used to working in the suburbs? Spend some time in urban settings. Again, this is about injecting fresh energy into your creative life.

You can also offer to teach your craft to those less fortunate. Volunteer at a prison, hospital or nursing home. View your creative life through the lens of someone in a challenging life situation and see how that touches your own life, how it impacts your work. This can be heart opening, and an open heart can bring forth lots of love-infused juice. More on this later.

Creative Story by Sarah Spector

"I weave into everything I see. Everything I see and experience is woven through me like a tapestry of song, of movement and of vision. I NEED TO CREATE. Everything I see is illuminated by pulsing life, by the joy of feeling and sensing, by the thrust of new life. Constantly.

This is my life. It's how I was born. I was born lucky in that I've always had some measure of support from family. Without this, life becomes struggle and loses its vibrancy.

When I can proceed naturally, meaning without material worry, I LIVE TO CREATE. Whether through painting or learning and mastering music, it's what unfolds my joy. It's who I am. It's like breathing.

In a state of relaxation. It's what I do. It's as simple as that. There's no formula except that - when not in a state of material struggle, I simply put my attention on doing it, and I do it. It's my life and my joy.

If I were to be without it (I have tried this), it would be as though I was underwater without air, or as if I was drained of blood. It's no fun.

Feeding this natural state of being is where I live (including the nature surrounding me), my friends and supporters (I am sustained by their friendship), regular movement and body care, and silence. Also, novelty, playfulness, exploration - studying and mastering new things, the daily adventure of living, making new acquaintances and new experiences - and maintaining homeostasis in terms of health and fitness.

Everything pulses with joyful life for me. I am sensual and vibrant. This is part of my joy - it's the vibrancy of everything."

FOLLOW THE ENERGY

Energy doesn't lie. Few of us pay attention to it except when we have too much or too little. Both have consequences, forcing us to see that we're out of balance.

Let's imagine for a moment, that we truly tuned into our energy levels and based our output around that. This would require us to observe how we feel at various times of the day and evening, noticing when we feel the most inspired and motivated and when we feel depleted or in need of rest. To really tap into the well of energy that fuels creative projects, we need to get to know how to prevent ourselves from burning out, so that we have plenty of juice left to carry us through the inner imaginative realms.

Question: What are at least two new ways you can get your creative juices going?

Activity of the Day: Observe your energy for a week, paying attention to when you feel the most inspired and motivated to work on a creative project. Whether you're a morning person or a night owl, structure your creative time around that time. Also, in response to the above question, try some new ways to boost your creative energy.

Inspiration of the Day: Watch Ted Talks on creativity.

13
SACRED SPACE

Your sacred space is where you can find yourself over and over again. — Joseph Campbell

Powerful women crave sacred space for luscious moments of self-care to balance all of the loving energy they generously give to others. — Shann Vander Leek

T̶HE CONTAINER IN WHICH YOU GROW AND BLOOM CREATIVELY matters as much as what you're creating. Having a space with the right energy, lighting, temperature, visual atmosphere, and appealing sounds and smells is essential to the creative process— it's the *sacred container* that holds your work. It's the rendezvous spot where you meet with your Muse, so you want it to be inspiring and supportive.

A good place to start is to determine if you can create a space where you live. If you share space with other people, a room where you can close the door is ideal. If you live alone, having a separate room can cut down on household distractions. A section of a room can also work. Creative use of room dividers provides privacy and segregation from the other aspects of your daily life.

If working at home isn't feasible, then, depending upon your mode of creative expression, you will need to seek out another space that will be conducive to your work. This can range from sharing a studio space, to jamming in a friend's garage, to working on a laptop in a café. What matters more than the specifics is how things flow in that space. Do you feel inspired or blocked? Is your energy expansive or contracted? Are you able to enter a zone that evokes joy making time disappear? Pay attention to the feel and the flow of a place until you find "your place".

Think you are stale or blocked creatively? It may be that you simply need a better space to work. A writer student of mine was frustrated and stuck. After exploring the issue for a while, I asked her about her writing space. She said she didn't feel comfortable writing at home because there were too many distractions and interruptions. I suggested writing at cafes or her local library. This small change opened the flow in her writing practice again.

CREATIVE STORY BY LIZ LABUNSKI

> "Growing up I was always interested in painting and drawing, however, life got in the way. Finding time to be creative took a back seat to raising my four children. Here and there I began to dabble in jewelry making, but mostly my focus during that time was on meeting the needs of my family.
>
> I live in a three-bedroom townhouse. For the first three out of five years that have I lived here, I kept my jewelry-making supplies tucked away in a big plastic container in my master bedroom closet with the idea that one day I would get it all out when I finally got a real studio.
>
> This became a creative barrier for me. Also, somewhat of an excuse.

Then in Jan of 2014, my sister, Victoria, (the author of this book) encouraged me to enroll in her online Creative Alchemy e-course. During the course, I discovered that I LOVED the way I felt when I honored my Muse! I finally felt that I had PERMISSION to let that side of myself out, and that I didn't need to go to a studio to get there.

I did create a sacred space during the course; just a small spot in my bedroom, tucked in a corner. I had my mason jars and my journal there, and the candles I lit while I was working during the course.

During that time, my beads and jewelry findings lived on the dining room table. I had fallen back in love with them and I decided I wasn't going to pack them up this time and put them or my creativity back in my master closet.

My bedroom is already a sanctuary for me; no television, lots of candles, incense, books, cozy fluffy pillows, and soft light. It's a peaceful and serene place. At first I hesitated to change anything about my little oasis, but then I thought, no, this is the PERFECT space for a small studio! I didn't need to travel to make art! I could make it right here!

As I cleared a space along a whole wall on the side of my bedroom, I got really excited. I took my Muse with me to Ikea to get a great workbench – a nice white plank with a bright yellow edge and two metal sawhorses—perfect for my little jewelry-making station! My sacred space was born!

In every spare moment, I began making lots of jewelry, created an online shop and began vending at festivals and events. Then last fall I took an art class in the NC mountains taught by a local artist from Charlotte. It was an intuitive paint and collage class. That class was yet another catalyst for awakening my creative self. Again, it opened the door to a side of myself I had closed. I felt I had finally given myself permission to reconnect with this part of me, and that at the heart of my being, I am a creative soul; an artist, and that I feel most alive when I am making something.

It has been almost four years since I created my little bedroom studio. I have practically outgrown it! I added another table to my studio area for paints and canvases, and I have spent many hours painting and making art in my sacred little space. My studio now has hundreds of beads as well as canvases, paints, sketchbooks and pencils.

Today, I am part of several online groups of artists who share their art through social media. I hope to someday submit some of my paintings to a gallery for a show. I am also in the process of adding some of my art pieces to my online shop."

Once you've settled on a space, the next step is to make it sacred. There are many ways to do this—it will be as individual as you are. The point is to create a sanctuary that feels clean, comfortable, beautiful, and inspiring! Some may disagree, arguing that they like disorder and chaos when they create, which is, of course, an individual preference. However, many of us (me included) thrive when certain qualities exist in our creative environments. Perhaps you agree, but I find that too much dirt, noise, clutter, and chaos evoke resistance in me.

Let's talk about clutter for a moment. Clutter in all its forms creates *visual noise*, as my friend Tracy, a professional organizer, likes to call it. It disrupts the flow of energy in a space, keeping things feeling tight, blocked, and restricted. The key is to have plenty of space without excess stuff. Ideally, before launching into a major project, make sure you clear out the space you'll be using so you can spread out and be organized.

ELEVATE THE VIBRATION

Once you've removed the clutter, you can set up a space that supports your creative expression. Start by elevating the vibration:

1. Clean entire space from top to bottom, including wiping down the walls

2. Use a sage wand to smudge the air (you can purchase one at Whole Foods or a new age bookstore).
3. You can also create a sage spray by mixing several drops essential oil with water in a spray bottle.
4. Open windows and doors and let fresh air move freely through the room.
5. Spend time meditating in the space.
6. Play high vibration ambient or classical music for 20 – 30 minutes. Music can completely retune the vibrations of the room.
7. Take a bath in Epsom salts to release toxins and cleanse yourself so that you don't bring negative energy into your creative space.

INVOLVE ALL OF YOUR SENSES

Once everything feels clean and spacious, you can add some personal touches that are meaningful to you:

- Essential oils with diffuser
- Fresh cut flowers and plants
- Candles and sacred objects
- Art by your favorite artists
- Framed poetry
- Precious stones
- Sound system for your favorite music
- Favorite teas and fresh water

WORKING OUTSIDE YOUR HOME

For those of you that write in cafés, you have an entirely different set of issues. You'll need to seek out places that not only have your favorite beverages and snacks, but also things like good lighting, comfortable seating, high speed Wi-Fi, and so on. More times than I can count, I've had to leave cafés because they just didn't feel right on a particular day. I'm super sensitive to energy, so I gauge if I'll be able to work in a place by how it feels. Sometimes it flows and sometimes it doesn't. Sometimes I café-hop from one place to another until I hit just the right mix for my mood and the type of writing I want to do. Ordering tea is cheaper than the higher end coffee drinks, so that's one way to keep the cost down. I don't mind paying for beverages because I see it as rent for the time I'm there.

There's no easy way to make a café space feel sacred; however, you can bring along some items that will make the table where you're working feel sacred, including a favorite journal, a small plant or flower, an unlit candle, stones or crystals, a small statue, a special scarf or other artsy or spiritual items. Consider it a mini altar that you carry with you. Setting an intention that the space is clean and clear before you arrive will also help make it feel sacred.

Question: What steps do you need to take to create a sacred space for your creative projects or elevate the vibrations of the one you currently have?

Activity: Create a sacred space for yourself to do your creative projects or find ways of elevating the vibrations of the space you already have.

Inspiration: Look up creative or sacred spaces on Pinterest.

14
CREATIVE RITUALS

We become what we behold. We shape our tools, and thereafter our tools shape us. — Marshall McLuhan

You have a destiny and a purpose that no one else on this earth can fulfill...and you have traveled a unique journey that has equipped you along the way with the tools you need to carry it out. — Mandy Hale

THE TOOLS OF CREATIVITY NOT ONLY INCLUDE YOUR SUPPLIES, BUT also the rituals that help you create. You may call what holds your creative process a ritual, routine, creative habit, strategy, tool, etc. Whatever you call it, it's what you need to do to support the creative flow. This is similar to the earlier chapter about befriending the Muse, however it goes a bit deeper. Sometimes, just going through the motions of setting up one's space and creating a checklist of inner preparations isn't enough. Sometimes we need to pause and listen again to see if we're truly dialed in or if we're just assuming that a particular way of doing things will work.

Better to try a few things, as I did when I bought my first laptop and timidly sat down at the café across the street from my house and started typing (I know, I didn't really go far from home that first time). It was painfully awkward at first, but after a few days, I began my first full-length screenplay. After several months, I finished the entire first draft in that same café. I was hooked! Writing at home was never the same after that.

Now whenever I'm in a café, especially one with couches and comfortable chairs, a well-brewed hot beverage and streaming music coming through my headphones, I can effortlessly move into the creative flow with my Muse. It's a good thing because when I lived nomadically for three years, that way of writing fit seamlessly into my new lifestyle.

Creative rituals, in a sense, set up a "muscle memory" or imprint of a particular set of environmental triggers that remind you that you are about to do something creative. It helps you overcome resistance and reduces the likelihood that you'll make up excuses and bail out.

Many books that offer advice on the creative process offer suggestions for ways to trick your mind into agreeing to do what you want to do, even if you are feeling reluctant or blocked. Why are these creative gymnastics even necessary? My viewpoint is that our struggles with creativity date back to our early years, when we entered school, where (for many of us), creativity was tucked away into small spaces of time in between "the more important" scholastic work. The world of work is no better. The same devaluing of creativity continues, causing it to be seen as impractical, indulgent, and insignificant.

Due to this lack of ongoing external support from the world around us, we must find tools and techniques that help us navigate our way through the inner creative landscape without the fear of being judged. In this sense, your Muse becomes your greatest ally. As you strengthen your relationship with her, she will carry you past the demons of doubt and negativity into the timeless joy of true self-expression. Once you taste the deliciousness of that, you'll want more and will do what it takes to access it.

How about you? What do you do to motivate, ground, and prepare yourself to step into the creative realm? If you don't have any regular tools or routines you use, perhaps you could adopt some fun activities that open your heart, your right-brain, and your flow so that when you begin, the faucet is already wide open. Stress and strain or too much pressure blocks the flow. Putting together a toolkit of strategies that keeps things moving is as important as having a sacred space.

Through trial and error, you'll eventually discover what makes the creative juices flow and what seems to stop them in their tracks. Often with both clients and students of mine, I've seen that sometimes just a simple shift in the way they approach their creative projects can get things moving.

When in doubt try a new way of doing things!

Question: What strategies or routines are part of your creative toolkit?
Activity: Make a list in your CA journal of strategies, routines, and even physical items you want to have in your toolkit.
Inspiration of the Day: Read "Sacred Mirrorism" by Alex Grey on his website.

15
DAILY PRACTICE

DAILY PRACTICE

In the realm of ideas everything depends on enthusiasm... in the real world all rests on perseverance. — Johann Wolfgang von Goethe

When I'm in writing mode for a novel, I get up at 4:00 am and work for five to six hours. In the afternoon, I run for 10km or swim for 1500m (or do both), then I read a bit and listen to some music. I go to bed at 9:00 pm. I keep to this routine every day without variation. The repetition itself becomes the important thing; it's a form of mesmerism. I mesmerize myself to reach a deeper state of mind. — Haruki Murakami

WE LIVE IN A TIME WITH SEEMINGLY ENDLESS OPPORTUNITIES AND choices. It's challenging amidst the many responsibilities and distractions that pull our attention to carve out regular creative time. If you're working, and have small children at home, it's especially difficult. However, people in all kinds of circumstances have managed to carve out time to create ample bodies of work.

. . .

How do they do it?

What makes them different from people who never seem to have time?

Forgive my bluntness, but it's quite simple: *those who do are in the habit of doing, while those who don't are in the habit of making excuses for not doing.* Over the years, I've heard *hundreds* of people complain that they don't have enough time to work on creative projects. Not true, I say. In a 24-hour period of time, we're all allotted the same amount of time to spend. What we do with that allotment is up to us. There is no one to blame when we waste or misuse it. Rather than beat ourselves up about it, why not look to those who've found a way through the inertia and see how they've managed to break through?

CREATIVE STORY BY SUZI POLAND

"*Simply turn up, every day and do something—one thing—on your creative journey. Small deposits into buckets, that one day overflow and tap wells—creativity to be shared with the world, when you and it are ready.*

Yes, this is my guiding philosophy, my approach to making art. Rather than finding it hard or tiring to go alone on a seemingly mysterious trail, soon to be depleted or give up, I somehow, some time ago, stumbled upon the concept and benefits of Personal Projects. Little creative containers that evolve and form in-tune with their contents and the creators who create them, the concepts they express and the consumers who eventually drink from them, enabling the creator to continue, to keep going, to keep turning up, to do it again and again.

This is how it's been for me, creating mini bodies of work that eventually tell me where they want to go. Like children, some are young and small, some still embryos waiting to be born, others are like older children ready to leave the nest and find their way in the world, to become a part of new tribes which are forming in collaboration with others.

Before we start engaging with others though, we must start with ourselves. Start with listening, really listening to what makes us happy, what fills us with love. Take a journal, keep a diary, a sketchbook, take a photo, make something, anything and capture it or jot it down. Hold it closely, create a safe haven, a safe space, a vessel for it to grow, until it speaks to you, tells you what it wants you to do, where it wants to go.

Begin with a certain time of day, in a certain way, with a certain medium, anything. Set a target, a number, an amount, and keep going until you finish or are bored. If you finish, do another, then another. Change it up, challenge yourself, do more, make it harder. Do it in a way you don't know how. If you get bored, give up, let it go and start another, or better still, keep them both going. Different rhythms, different themes.

I'm a plate spinner, not a mountain climber. Lots of different projects on the go. Some people like to master things, climb to the peak, climb down, then start again. I like to work seasonally, revisiting the same things with fresh eyes, always adding to the work I've done before.

Now, having worked this way for over six years, some things are ready to go to exhibition, others to print. Some still need protecting, nurturing, listening to. More time to grow. They simply are not ready.

Others, the older ones, the faster ones, the simpler ones, the more advanced ones, are ready to go, ready for the challenges ahead. I am ready too, but I won't be left destitute when they go, depleted, exhausted, not sure where to go, with no idea what to do next.

It may be unusual to work this way, I don't know, but it's my way, a way that works for me, sustains me, sustains my art. Keeps me creating in a variety of ways that holds my interest and excitement, allows my self-expression.

Sometime later, after you've mastered a Personal Project, it's possible to begin a Shared Project or a Public Project but they are not for the faint hearted. You will need support from others to help you and before you gain that, you need to know yourself, know how you work, know what you can't do, what you struggle with. That's when you can offer the hand of friendship, creative kin-ship, combing in collaboration.

Until then, make art for yourself and enjoy it. That's an achievement in itself."

A bit of research into the lives of successful artists reveals one thing: they all found the time to make their art. Perhaps it is more accurate to say they all *made* the time to create, with most doing so daily. Ideally, you too, would want to have creativity be a part of your daily life. Personally, I prefer viewing my creative time as a *daily practice* because that way each day I have a new opportunity to choose it again. Plus, if you practice something long enough, you'll not only have a degree of mastery, but also a new habit!

If the words daily practice seem daunting, then perhaps the words creative habit—as the dancer Twyla Tharp calls it in her book by the same name—would be a better way to identify the regular hours you spend each week on your creativity. Go with whatever resonates with you. In my case, I have a daily spiritual practice and the idea of folding my creativity right into that appeals to me—the two are compatible, and both benefit from daily attention.

To assist you with this process, let's explore some activities from which you might be able to *borrow or steal time*. My intention is not to make you feel guilt or shame, but to show you just how much extra time you might have.

If you don't believe me, take this short quiz:

- How many hours per day do you spend watching television? Per week?
- How many hours per day do you spend playing computer games? Per week?
- How many hours per day do you spend playing games on your phone? Per week?
- How many hours per day do you spend texting and talking on the phone? Per week?
- How many hours per day do you spend on Facebook and other social media? Per week?
- How many hours per day do you spend on other unnecessary activities? Per week?

Add these hours up and you'll discover that you have some currency to draw upon when setting aside time to be creative. Don't be too hard on yourself. I'm the first to admit, I've struggled with this issue for years. During most of my married life while raising two children, my family depended on me for income, so I was always extraordinarily busy. Having a writing group to support me became a lifesaver of my creative life. And yet, the negative gremlins would still sneak in here and there to point out that I wasn't writing enough. Sometimes, when I look back and I'm being especially hard on myself, I admit that I feel as though I let myself down by not prioritizing my writing enough. I tell myself, I could have done so much more. Then my inner wise woman comes forth and shows me the futility of that type of thinking. It's not kind. It's not loving. It's not helpful. I can't go back and change the past. I can only do what I can right now.

And so can you.

Remember, new habits take time to cultivate. Those that stick are the ones that are anchored by commitment and accountability. Commitment may be as simple as making appointments with yourself and writing them on the calendar. Accountability may take the form of a creative buddy, a coach, a writing group or setting yourself up with some important deadlines that require you to finish a project. Regardless of how you decide to anchor your habit, do your best to find ways to make space in your life for a regular infusion of the magical, untamed, artsy side of life. It can truly transform the dreariest of days when you show up and invite the Muse to play.

BENEFITS OF ESTABLISHING A DAILY CREATIVE PRACTICE

- Consistency in our work
- Momentum that keeps us moving forward
- Staying connected with a project even when we're not working on it
- Keeps the energy high and exciting
- A feeling of accomplishment
- A sense of mastery as our skills grow and expand
- An inner knowing that our priorities are more balanced
- Freedom from excuses and procrastination

- Establishes the character to hold our gifts including discipline, patience and commitment

Question: What are some excuses you currently use to get out of working on your creative projects?

Activity: Now that you've made time with your Muse, consider taking the next step and see how you might establish a regular creative habit. If you work full time, can you schedule a few lunch hours to do some sketching or journaling or taking photographs. You could also take a walk and record some ideas. If you don't work full time, when are the best times in your day to block off chunks of time? Ideally, you want to follow the energy. Some people have lots of energy in the morning, while others are night owls. Regardless of when it is, set the intention to shift from random creative bursts to a regular schedule if not every day, then at least three times per week minimum. Better to do regular, consistent, small bursts, than occasional big bursts.

Inspiration: Read *The Creative Habit: Learn it and Use it For Life* by Twyla Tharp.

PART IV

LISTEN TO LIFE

LISTEN TO LIFE

When a coincidence arises, don't ignore it. Ask yourself, What is the message here? What is the significance of this? You don't need to go digging for the answers. Ask the question, and the answers will emerge. They may arrive as a sudden insight, a spontaneous creative experience, or they may be something very different. Perhaps you will meet a person who is somehow related to the coincidence that occurred. An encounter, a relationship, a chance meeting, a situation, a circumstance will immediately give you a clue to its meaning. "Oh, so that's what it was all about!" — Deepak Chopra

The concept of randomness and coincidence will be obsolete when people can finally define a formulation of patterned interaction between all things within the universe. — Toba Beta

IN THIS SECTION, WE'LL FOCUS ON THE WAY LIFE COMMUNICATES. Everywhere we look there are myriad ways that life speaks to us. Though it may appear that we're separate, we're all connected.

Therefore, when something occurs in our world, it's connected to the whole, and, as a result, there is meaning behind every thought, word, and deed...every incident and every act.

Of course, we cannot possibly pay attention to every little thing. What we can do is tune into our surroundings and the people in them—we can pick up non-verbal clues that may answer questions, solve problems, give us direction, open a new perspective, inspire a decision, and so on.

In the Western world, unlike that of our indigenous brothers and sisters, we're not raised to give heed to these signs and messages. Once we're in school, our early childhood connection with that innate ability to sense, feel, and know things on a non-verbal level begins to fade. Because it's not cultivated, it grows dormant. A fortunate few are raised in families that value intuition and an empathic way of relating to the world. For the rest of us, we must consciously decide to make it a priority and spend time learning to use this tool.

Unfortunately, following one's intuition is often discouraged and frowned upon by the people around us. It's foreign, and therefore, much doubt and second-guessing surrounds its implementation. The exception to this occurs when there's a crisis or emergency; then this unused capacity gets rapidly activated to assist with survival. In those circumstances, there is less scrutiny, making it easier to simply follow through on that gut instinct.

In day-to-day life, it's altogether different. Though we face lots of choices that would benefit greatly from listening to the subtle messages communicated by the world around us, we often miss the clues. Life regularly offers us guidance, but for the most part we don't trust ourselves enough to listen. Instead, we let fear inform our decisions—choosing security and safety, rather than face the risk of an unknown outcome. We often do this even when we suspect that listening to life's nudges might be better for us in the long run and answer our dreams of a better life.

Lucky for us, life is patient. It keeps calling on us and doesn't give up. It's always waiting for us to pay attention. And when we don't, we're only hurting ourselves.

I would go so far as to say that when we really listen, life—as guided by our intuition—*never* lets us down. This is not true of our intellect and emotions. Decisions made solely from those aspects of ourselves usually have consequences and end badly.

I liken the guidance of life to a wise sage (we'll explore this in the chapter on intuition), whereas I see my mind or intellect as a naïve apprentice. Seeing it this way makes the difference obvious, doesn't it? Basically, the mind works fine when I *clearly* tell it what I need. It is an assistant or tool, but it was never meant to lead. But I've learned the hard way that it's not wise to let it run my life. Better instead to rely on a sacred mix of intuition and intellect that draws on a higher wisdom from within.

How about you? Are you ready to deepen your listening skills?

REFLECTION QUESTION

In what areas of your life would you like to pay more attention?

BEFORE WE BEGIN

- Set an intention for this section.
- Reflect on a time when life spoke to you when you DID listen and reflect on a time when life spoke to you when you DID NOT listen.
- Choose one of the four areas (dreams, signs and signals, intuition, body wisdom) in this section to invest some time cultivating your listening skills.

16
DREAMS

I've dreamt in my life dreams that have stayed with me ever after, and changed my ideas: they've gone through and through me, like wine through water, and altered the colour of my mind. — Emily Bronte

I dream my paintings, then I paint my dreams. — Vincent van Gogh

ARTISTS, WRITERS, MUSICIANS, AND OTHER CREATIVE GENIUSES throughout history have tapped into the phantasmagorical and mythological elements of dreams to create masterpieces that could not have been fathomed by ordinary waking consciousness. Capturing bits and pieces of this realm infuses the creative world with the unusual, the extraordinary, and the transpersonal.

The world of dreams is the domain of the mysterious and the surreal—the land of imagination gone wild. It is the arena in which we work out our unexpressed fears, desires, and ideas. It is also where we receive messages from our unconscious. Sometimes they come in the form of a warning or premonition. Other times, we receive a symbolic or archetypal vision that answers a question, solves a problem or hints at a new direction. And other times, we simply find ourselves in extraordinary circumstances, helping us transcend our human limitations, even if just for a brief period.

I've always loved the way Native Americans use dream-catchers to protect the dreamer from negative dreams while allowing positive dreams through. Unfortunately, we've lost much of the significance placed on dreams and their meaning by both ancient as well as indigenous cultures.

To show just how deep these roots go, here are a few tidbits I found on author and dream analyst, Tony Crisp's website:

- In ancient Egypt, dreams were interpreted by temple priests who regarded dreams as messengers.
- The Greeks gave us our first dream dictionary written around 140 AD by Artemidorus of Daldis.
- Native Americans access the world of dreams for decision-making and as part of their sacred rituals.
- Aborigines, who don't view death as the end, acknowledge that ancestors visit us through our dreams and can offer us healing.

That's just a small sampling of the ways in which certain cultures have viewed the power of dreams. In the creative ecosphere, dreams can be a wonderfully fertile source of inspirational fodder, providing us with simple things such as titles of books, lyrics for a song, the name of a character, an idea for a sketch, etc. However, we shouldn't underestimate this simplicity. These sacred gifts usually have a lot of energy behind them when they come through our dreams, which is perhaps due to our greater receptivity when we're sleeping. When we're shut off from the world and released from its grip, we have access to an abundance of ingredients we can ultimately integrate into the world of form.

A POWERFUL MESSENGER

Dreams are such a profound, innate resource, and yet many of us don't utilize them much, if at all. If you do, good for you! You're the exception. For those of you who don't, I encourage you to begin paying attention to them so that you can access a boundless source of new inspiration!

Here are some basic steps to help you connect with the dream world:

1. Before you fall asleep, set an intention that you will remember your dreams.
2. Keep a dream journal or pen and paper near your bed, and record your dreams upon waking.
3. Use dream interpretation tools or archetypes to understand the messages contained within your dreams.
4. Incorporate the images, words, sounds, ideas, feelings, message, etc. from your dream journal into your creative work.
5. Learn about lucid dreaming so that you can take a more active role in your dreams.
6. Spend time during the day allowing yourself to daydream and write down your experiences with that.
7. Share your dreams with others. This makes them more vivid and easier to remember.

Question: How can you bring more of your dream world into your creative world?

Activity: Find a special notebook or journal that you will use to record your dreams. Before you go to bed at night or lie down to rest during the day, put a pen and paper next to you. After you lie down, mentally ask your intuition for a dream or daydream image that will benefit your creative life. When you wake up, even if you don't remember anything specific, write or draw whatever comes into your mind. Find ways to use some of your dreams in your creative expression.

Inspiration: Explore the magical world of dreams by doing some of your own research and by reading books and watching videos by dream experts.

17
SIGNS AND SIGNALS

When we're interested in something, everything around us appears to refer to it (the mystics call these phenomena "signs," the skeptics "coincidence," and psychologists "concentrated focus," although I've yet to find out what term historians should use). — Paulo Coelho

Synchronicity is an ever present reality for those who have eyes to see. — Carl Jung

FIRST DESCRIBED BY CARL GUSTAV JUNG IN THE 1920S, WIKIPEDIA defines synchronicity as "the experience of two or more events as meaningfully related, where they are unlikely to be causally related. The subject sees it as a meaningful coincidence, although the events need not be exactly simultaneous in time."

A meaningful coincidence. A happy accident. A fortuitous event. A stroke of luck. Being in the right place at the right time. These are some of the ways we describe a synchronistic event. I also call it a sign, signal, nudge or message from life.

Synchronicity may also be connected to our unconscious desires, so it looks as though the coincidences are happening "to us" instead of as a direct reflection of our own inner desires and intentions made manifest. Synchronistic events are one way our soul or Higher Self communicates with us; they can be a powerful "heads-up," calling us to pay attention. I'm sure many of these have occurred in your own life.

According to Trish and Rob MacGregor, authors of *The 7 Secrets of Synchronicity* (Adams, 2010), "A synchronicity can serve as guidance, warning, affirmation, creative inspiration, confirmation that we're on the right track. It can be evidence of individuation and psychological growth. Or it can simply serve to attune our awareness that beneath the surface of daily life there's an underlying reality and unity that may not be immediately obvious."

This is yet another confirmation that life speaks to us all the time. It's continually sending us messages in a variety of ways: a chance meeting with someone, a song on the radio, a street sign, a passage in a book, a conversation with a friend, and so on. Sometimes the messages are gentle nudges; sometimes they're wake-up calls that appear in the form of a near accident, sudden illness, stroke of bad luck, feeling of being out of the flow, etc.

Now consider how useful it might be to pause when something out of the ordinary happens in your life and ask the following questions:

1. Has your life been speaking to you lately? If so, is it whispering or is it shouting?
2. Are you listening to these whispers, hints, clues, and messages or are you ignoring them?
3. Are you acting on what you hear or are you delaying or avoiding action?
4. What do you think the universe wants from you right now?

5. How can you demonstrate that you are open and listening?

BEING PRESENT & RECEPTIVE

In the same way that recording your dreams may enrich your artistic expression, being receptive to the way life communicates with you can help you to feel more connected to the whole. Each moment of your life then becomes jam-packed with the potential to teach you, guide you, inspire you, and motivate you to draw buckets of wisdom from this infinite well.

These signs and symbols tend to show up most often when you're open, humble, and in sync with life's flow. This means loosening your need to control things. It also means relating to life more as a partnership rather than an external force to manage.

Practicing being in the present helps, as does slowing down. Meditation is another wonderful way to set aside time to tune your channel to your Muse. Distractions and drama create lots of static and noise, making it difficult to notice when life tries to get your attention. If your Muse speaks in whispers, you'll need to get really quiet to hear what she wants to tell you.

When we listen to and heed the messages, life rewards us with even more messages. Our world becomes alight with passion fueled by the very Source of our existence. It's confirmation that life is conspiring for our highest joy—we only need to listen to feel connected to that ever-present support.

Unfortunately, we sometimes get in the way of that reciprocal interchange, and end up feeling cut off from that flow, alone and bewildered. It's as if we're in the middle of a foreign city overrun with noise and chaos and we've lost our GPS signal. It doesn't feel good!

STEP BACK INTO THE FLOW

The good news is that we can always correct our course. We can step back into that flow with life. First, we must admit we're off course. Second, we need to slow down enough to tune in. Third, once we hear the inner guidance again, we need to follow it. Finally, it is important to show our gratitude for the messages life gives us. Gratitude opens our hearts, which in turn, connects us to our natural state: love.

Question: What's the most powerful example of synchronicity or coincidence that ever happened to you?

Activity: Pay attention to signs, signals, messages, serendipity, and meaningful coincidences in your life. Write what you notice in your CA journal.

Inspiration: Read *The Field: The Quest for the Secret Force of the Universe* by Lynne McTaggart.

18
INTUITION

We all have an inner voice, our personal whisper from the universe. All we have to do is listen -- feel and sense it with an open heart. Sometimes it whispers of intuition or precognition. Other times, it whispers an awareness, a remembrance from another plane. Dare to listen. Dare to hear with your heart. — C.J. Heck, author of *Bit and Pieces: Short Stories from a Writer's Soul*

Nothing comes unannounced, but many can miss the announcement. So it's very important to actually listen to your own intuition rather than driving through it. — Terence McKenna

INTUITION HAS MANY QUALITIES, BUT IT STILL ISN'T ALWAYS EASY TO recognize or follow its guidance. Initially, when it first comes in, it often manifests as feelings, scattered energy, a knowing sense, a vague nudge or unease. It can be tricky interpreting what's coming through. It resembles the fuzzy feeling associated with remembering a dream. Despite this fuzziness, there's usually a strong feeling that something important is stirring us from within. It's the particular combination of feelings and the intensity around it that distinguishes it from something coming from the intellect.

SOME DESCRIPTIVE STATEMENTS ABOUT INTUITION

- Intuition is our inner GPS.
- Intuition is our best friend and ally.
- Intuition can solve any problem or difficulty.
- Intuition can lead us to experiences and opportunities otherwise unavailable to us.
- Intuition provides us with an infinite supply of deep universal wisdom.
- Intuition opens the way for the Highest Good.
- Intuition is the way of the heart.
- Intuition connects us with the Source of all that is.

It takes practice to truly discern intuitive guidance from the other voices competing for our attention—a slippery slope until we can fully grasp that there is indeed a difference.

How is this done?

One simple technique is to see yourself having inner and outer channels at any given time. Your intuition is one of these channels. Since the reception may be faint, then it will necessitate blocking out the noise around you so that you can hear it. When you feel a tug or nudge, see if you can stop what you're doing for a moment, then see what comes through.

CREATIVE STORY BY SUZANNE MCRAE

"Years ago, during a long bout of insomnia, I spent quiet nighttime hours in prayer and doing Reiki. During that time, my intuitive voice began speaking to me more clearly. I also felt a deeper connection to my heart and soul, and that brought me to a peaceful place.

The intuitive voice would prove to be helpful in ways I had not even imagined. During one of those sleepless nights I found a lump in my breast. The alarm bells were ringing so loud inside of me that I thought it would wake up my family. But even in those moments of sheer panic and fear, I knew what had to happen next. It was clear. A short while later I was diagnosed with breast cancer.

The diagnosis left me feeling like I was a ship lost at rough sea. It was the start of a very scary journey where the descent felt steep, deep, filled with darkness and uncertainty. I felt so alone, but I would soon enough discover that I was not.

My muse's presence came on board fairly early on to support me. Her soft, gentle presence brought me to a place where I was able to feel more connected and present. Where the greater truths and wisdom inside of me would reveal themselves.

I often sense my muse taking me by the hand and leading me to a place where it feels like a protective cocoon. A place where there is a deep feeling of peace and calm. She loves to make me colour, go on nature walks, and explore photography and writing. She knows the perfect scenario to get me out of the intensity that I can feel at times. She is very good at getting me back into my creative process, that place where nothing else matters but what's happening in the moment.

When I colour she brings me back to my child-like place, where I see a world filled with colours that automatically opens me up to seeing so many more possibilities of healing. When she notices the anxiety and panic beginning to appear for me, she will bring me to the forest to spend time with the trees, streams and God. In photographing nature, I *capture the beauty of all there is, whether it be in the forest or within me.*

My muse brought me back to writing and sharing through my blog about my experience with cancer. It has been incredibly difficult to do, because I have felt so vulnerable and raw in the process of living with cancer. But writing has given me greater access to even deeper parts of myself, where the pain hides, and that all needs to come on board for greater healing to take place. I am so grateful to my intuition and muse for how they are guiding and supporting me."

CLUES TO HELP YOU RECOGNIZE YOUR INTUITION

- **Tone.** The voice of intuition, which you may call your Higher Self, Source or God, has a calm, wise, emotionally neutral tone like that of a beloved grandparent. The voices of the mind—sometimes referred to as monkey mind—have a chaotic, frenetic, even emotionally charged tone that is ever-changing, and in a moment's notice can shift from rebellious child to scolding parent.
- **Content.** The voice of intuition tends to bring us information, insights, and wisdom that we need right now in our lives. It can be very simple, but it usually brings clarity to a specific situation. Other times, it might be more complex, helping to shift our perspective entirely or guide us to make a major decision in our life. The content of the mind, on the other hand, is all over the place. The messages are inconsistent and confusing, leading us in circles, rather than offering solutions. It has a reactive, impulsive quality to it that is often full of judgment or demands.

- **The State of Being Evoked.** The voice of intuition brings us feelings of expansiveness, plus relief from finally having the vision to see the bigger picture. It's heart-opening and gifts us with compassion, forgiveness, and trust. The egoistic mind brings feelings of contraction and limitation. It makes us feel powerless and helpless, which we quickly attempt to cover up with a false sense of self-righteousness. Either way, the result is that those thoughts make us feel less than or more than others.
- **Intention.** Our intuition has our best interest at heart, while the mental monkey is only interested in survival at any cost.

Looking at the differences, there's no question which one we'd rather trust. The key is making the commitment to tune into it. With practice, hearing this inner voice becomes second nature, and it takes on the qualities of a companion that's always with us when we need it, wherever we need it, lighting our way through the unknown.

Question: How can you honor and strengthen your intuition?
Activity: Close your eyes and focus on your breath. Breathe gently and consciously, releasing all thoughts, concerns, distractions—just let them go and bring your focus to the present, to this room. Now, identify an event or situation that you'd like more insight about. Ask yourself, "What does my life need right now?" Repeat the question another time or two if needed, then spend a few moments listening to what comes through. When you've finished, open your eyes. Write or draw your answer in your journal. Write whatever word or image comes up...don't stop to think, just let it flow.

Inspiration: Search for articles about intuition on the Brain Pickings website.

BODY WISDOM

The body is wiser than its inhabitants. the body is the soul. the body is god's messenger. — Erica Jong

But if one observes, one will see that the body has its own intelligence; it requires a great deal of intelligence to observe the intelligence of the body. — Jiddu Krishnamurti

OUR BODIES ARE THE INSTRUMENTS THROUGH WHICH WE experience the world, and specifically, the means through which we're able to bring our ideas into form. But how much do we truly connect with our body's wisdom?

In his book, *The Way of the Peaceful Warrior*, Dan Millman's teacher, Socrates, introduces him to the idea of body wisdom, when he tells him, "Everything you'll ever need to know is within you; the secrets of the universe are imprinted on the cells of your body. But you haven't learned inner vision; you don't know how to read the body. Your only recourse has been to read books and listen to experts and hope they are right."

We mistakenly place more value on the knowledge that comes from outside of us, than what comes from within. In our ignorance, we're missing out on one of life's greatest gifts.

A SACRED TEMPLE

The body is not just a machine to keep us alive and give us sensory information about the world we live in; it's much more than that. Indeed, it's a sacred temple that connects us to inner truth and wisdom. When our minds are running around like wild animals and our emotions have gone haywire, it is the body that can ground us in what's happening in the moment.

Just as most of us aren't accustomed to listening to our dreams and intuition, we're also not used to placing our trust in the body. Instead, we favor the intellect, and much to our own peril, we're cut off from our body's wisdom.

How do we change that? How do we read the body? How do we learn to listen to its messages? How do we reconnect with the wisdom it has to offer?

LISTENING TO OUR BODIES

If we consider the physical to be a barometer of our inner state of being, then listening to our bodies can teach us a lot about how we're doing. The physical is usually the last place something manifests, meaning energy flows first through the filter of our thoughts, then our emotions, until it finally arrives in the body.

The body, like the Muse, doesn't like to be ignored.

In fact, if we ignore the body long enough, it rebels and eventually stages an all-out revolution, stopping at nothing until it gets our attention. This is what might be called *a late-stage warning*. If a deep inner issue makes its way to the physical with lots of pain and discomfort, it's probably been there a long time—our ability to ignore whatever message is coming through has come to an end. We have reached a point at which we must pay attention.

Ideally, it would be better to listen to our body wisdom long before it turns into a full-blown crisis. It's a powerful tool that can guide us and help us make key decisions in our lives, preventing such crises. It can also be a partner in grounding our imaginations so we can move with ease between the imaginative realms and the physical realm of our daily lives.

TRY IT FOR YOURSELF

In any given situation, take a moment and scan your body. Tune into the visceral sensations you're feeling. Is your heart open or closed? It is beating normally or racing? Is your body tingling with excitement or trembling with fear? Is your jaw relaxed or is it tense? Are your hands open or clenched? Is your stomach loose or is it tight? Now, examine what you're thinking or doing. Are they in sync? Consider making a decision based only on what you're thinking. Then consider making a decision based only on the sensations you feel. Is there a difference? Would you make a different decision after scanning your body than you would have if you just listened to your logical mind?

Of course, most of us do this already without thinking about it. However, by becoming conscious of it, you'll discover that your decisions tend to be a more authentic reflection of your whole being, rather than just what you think you "should" do or what might conform to what others expect of you.

This is the beginning of true freedom.

. . .

Tuning into your body can shift the way you show up in your life. It can help you feel loved and nurtured. It can empower your sense of connectedness with Mother Earth. It can help you remain centered in the middle of chaos.

DELICIOUS WAYS TO TUNE INTO YOUR BODY

- Dance and other forms of movement
- Long, luxurious soaks in the tub
- Walking barefoot in the grass or sand
- Receiving a massage
- Self-care rituals such as salt rubs, facials, mani-pedi, conditioning treatments for your hair, etc.
- Meditation
- Conscious breathing techniques
- Stretching and yoga
- Cleanses and juice feasting
- Warming your body in a sauna

Most importantly, give your body's wisdom equal time and input into your creative process and your life. See it as one of your trusty guides responsible for taking the temperature of your life and providing you regular feedback regarding the state of your thoughts, emotions, beliefs, etc.

One last morsel ... don't forget to say thank you! Your body *loves* being appreciated for everything it does for you!

Question: How do you honor the sacredness of your body?
Activity: Spend some time tuning into your body. Listen to it. Ask it what it needs from you. Ask it if it has any message for you. Become receptive and present. Do some deep breathing, using either alternate nostril breathing, slow inhaling and exhaling...counting to 7 as you inhale, hold and counting 7 as you exhale, hold and repeat, or any other form of conscious breathing you'd like. Do a guided meditation that focuses on body relaxation. Take an Epsom salt bath to detox your body. Do some gratitude practice with a focus on your body, appreciating how much it supports you and your creativity. Think of other ways you can honor your sacred temple.
Inspiration: Read the poem, "The Spirit Likes to Dress Up" by Mary Oliver.

20
NATURE'S MEDICINE

The earth has music for those who listen. — George Santayana

The clearest way into the Universe is through a forest wilderness. — John Muir

DURING MY THREE YEARS TRAVELING AS A DIGITAL NOMAD, I WROTE A couple of blog posts about the intense relationship I have with trees. This love affair with trees was always present, but once I spent so much time on the road, my appreciation for their role in my life deepened. No longer seeing them as simply beautiful or merely supplying me with oxygen, I began to appreciate them as medicine for my soul and a sanctuary away from the man-made troubles of the world. This is not new, but it taught me to recognize a soul-feeding experience when I felt one. Now I recognize the call deep inside of me that pulls me outdoors to cleanse my head, purify my heart, and uplift my spirit.

The creative life is easily fueled by a strong relationship with nature as demonstrated by so many of our favorite poets, painters, and musicians whose work is infused with its earthly charm. Indeed, certain mystics and sages experienced major shifts in consciousness from studying the movements of an animal or watching the cycles of a plant.

Tuning into these subtle rhythms surrounding us can provide us with an endless supply of insight and wisdom. In fact, unplugging for long stretches of time helps us to withdraw and hit the reset button.

The Muse cannot compete with lots of external noise. She's more likely to appear amid the quiet sound of buzzing bees and birdsong than the blaring of the television. Needing significant periods of quiet and downtime is yet another way that the path of the artist resembles that of the mystic.

Nature is a wonderful way to spend that downtime. Worldly pursuits as well as creative pursuits require so much output from us that it's a blessing to spend time tuning into the music of birds, bees, and ground creatures. The simplicity returns our consciousness to a more innocent state, which softens our hearts. A soft, open heart is a gentle, trusting heart that feels peace in what is. The walls of protection and shielding come down, senses prickle with aliveness, and our awareness sharpens. All are qualities conducive to creativity.

There is even a practice in Japan called Shinrin-yoku, which in English means forest bathing. It is considered a powerful way to reduce stress and restore health through breathing in the medicinal, organic compounds that are emanated from trees.

In addition, in many cultures, the appearance of animals and their specific characteristics are considered bearers of messages. Viewing them that way opens us to the subtle, less visible energies that occur all around us, connecting us to the greater intelligence of Life. Instead of seeing ourselves as separate, nature continually invites us to recognize our connection to the whole, as well as our part within it.

Nature helps us find ourselves when feeling we're out of sorts.

It has the uncanny ability to restore our sanity right when we think we cannot handle another intrusion on our psyches. There is no judgment there, no pressure to perform, no expectations to do anything.

Observing the movements and patterns in nature are also great reminders to keep it simple, slow down, be present, and love without conditions. This aligns perfectly with our Muse, who wants nothing more than to cultivate these qualities in us. When our instrument is clean, the output of creative ideas can flow unimpeded.

Question: How does nature speak to you?
Activity: Spend time in nature tuning into your surroundings. Slow down and notice the small details: the sights, smells, sounds, and how it makes you feel. See yourself as intrinsically connected with everything around you. Allow your heart to open and soften. Ask a question or ask for a sign or clue that might answer a problem you're wrestling with. See what shows up. It may be subtle or it may be obvious. It may be quiet and slow in coming or it may be quick and fast. Allow it to be however it is. Invite your Muse into the quiet. Share it with her. Carry the energy from this experience back with you into your creative space.
Inspiration: Read *The Nature Fix: Why Nature Makes Us Happier, Healthier, and More Creative* by Florence Williams.

PART V

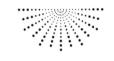

FIND YOUR VOICE

FIND YOUR VOICE

Don't try to figure out what other people want to hear from you; figure out what you have to say. It's the one and only thing you have to offer. — Barbara Kingsolver

The voice of our original self is often muffled, overwhelmed, even strangled, by the voices of other people's expectations. — Julia Cameron

WE ARE EACH WHOLLY UNIQUE—WE MAY RESONATE WITH OTHERS and share similar values, but our experience and perception of life are distinctly our own. This is exciting and sometimes terrifying, especially when it comes to expressing that uniqueness. Human beings are wired to conform and to seek acceptance and approval from others. Our survival has depended on this conformity for thousands of years. And yet, we also long to be loved and accepted for who we really are, unconditionally without our masks and props, without our story. We long to step out from behind the persona we've adopted to fit in and to make others comfortable—to be real, to be who we are.

As creative spirits, we may need to go through a period of

imitation of what we see out there, so that we can master the skills needed to express our gifts. But eventually the time comes for us to expand and evolve, moving away from the safety of the world of the known into the realm of the never-before-seen, into the deep waters of the original, the untold, the unexpressed.

As we explored in the beginning of the book, this takes courage. To express one's truth without pre-approval is a big, vulnerable step. To share what is uniquely coming through you in a way that is pure and without censorship is radical and empowering. To be who you are without fear of others' opinions is outrageous and enlivening.

It also gives others permission to do the same.

I'm in awe (as I'm sure you are) of those amazing artists out there that pull out all the stops while sharing their innermost souls without hesitation. The energy around their work is electric because it feels so fresh and newly born! It may shock, amuse, or dazzle us, but mostly, it paves the way for us to see the infinite world of possibilities that await us. All we need to do is tap into it, welcome it, and be willing to midwife it into existence.

What's beautiful is that as it emerges through us, we can also witness its movement from the formless into the world of form. It is truly a birth when it comes from this eternal, primordial place. How wonderful and awe-inspiring to be part of it!

FINDING YOUR VOICE

So how can you find your voice? There are multitudes of ways, but here are some suggestions:

1. Observe the patterns and themes that show up in your creative work.
2. Follow the energy. Notice where the greatest energy

around your creative work lies. Pay close attention to what enlivens you and brings you joy.
3. Get in touch with your values, convictions, and preferences. Create lists of what you love, what you believe, what matters to you, what inspires you, etc.
4. Take a break from looking at the creative work of others for a period of time and spend more time listening to and following what comes from within. The outside world of distractions and noise can make it difficult to filter out the influences and values of others.
5. Ask others what specific themes and values they notice in your work. Ask them how they would describe your style and the energy of your work.
6. Spend time in silence, just listening, watching, and being. See what arises in that space and calls for your attention.
7. Reflect on which books, movies, art, music, etc., really resonate and touch your soul. Study the creators behind those works. Hints and clues to your voice can be found there.

Once found, how can you strengthen that voice?

As with anything else, strength and mastery come with practice. Through cultivating a relationship with your Muse, you open the pathways to a deeper, more universal source of ideas. This doesn't mean that your story or signature isn't part of this universal expression. Instead, *you can extract the universal truth from within your own story.* Or to put it another way, you can take specific elements of your story and make it universal. It's simply a bigger way to hold your ideas. In a sense, you cease focusing on creating art for personal satisfaction or gain, but simply show up because it's a big part of who you are—it's a way of giving back to life.

All of us are, in a sense, living primarily to be used by life, gifting it with meaning, beauty, inspiration, and love. The payoff is that we get to spend time doing what we love, experiencing joy when our creative efforts touch someone's life.

Eventually, speaking your truth and doing art that reflects who you are will be as natural as breathing.

In the meantime...

Trust
Show up
Listen
Honor
Express
Appreciate

REFLECTION QUESTION

What step can you take right now to find and honor your creative voice?

BEFORE WE BEGIN

- Set an intention for this section.
- Set aside some time this week getting to know your creative essence or signature. How would you describe this essence?
- Explore ways to cultivate your own unique style of expression.

21
PERMISSION TO LOVE YOURSELF

The snow goose need not bathe to make itself white. Neither need you do anything but be yourself. — Lao Tzu

I now see how owning our story and loving ourselves through that process is the bravest thing that we will ever do. — Brené Brown

WHY IS THERE SO MUCH SELF-SABOTAGE OF OUR DEEPEST LONGING TO express ourselves creatively? We back burner the song in our hearts, sometimes for years at a time. Often it comes down to one thing: *the permission to love ourselves.* At an early age, we're made to feel guilty if we spend too much time in the world of fantasy and daydreams. As we get older, the pressure to be practical and focused on the outer world grows, while our connection to the Muse shrivels from neglect. We lose touch with our natural curiosity and love of learning. However, creativity is an essential part of who we are; we cannot live fully without that part of ourselves.

We all need to nourish ourselves—take time out, recharge, and restore. So many of us live on a self-starvation diet, depleting our stores of energy in exchange for money or some other commodity, that we've forgotten what really listening to our own needs even feels like.

Too much compromise makes us cranky. Long periods of habitual self-betrayal wear deep grooves in our psyches, leaving us depressed, angry or full of anxiety. Allowed to go on long enough, this depletion creates fertile ground for a major illness, meltdown or both.

This does not bode well for cultivating a vibrant creative life.

WHAT TO DO?

Take a long, deep breath, step back from your life and assess the damage. Ask yourself a few direct questions. Answer them in your CA journal, if you like.

1. In what areas of your life are you betraying yourself?
2. In what areas of your life do you deny your needs in favor of another's?
3. In what areas of your life is it more important to be liked than to follow your own way?
4. How much of yourself do you sacrifice (negotiate) to get something you want or hang onto something you have?

One way to stop the madness is by simply practicing the fine art of saying, "no" to as many people as you can get away with for as long as it takes to break the habit of saying, "Yes" when you'd rather not.

Another way is to pay attention to your body's energy levels. If something drains the crap out of you, by all means, don't do it. If it energizes and excites you, obviously keep doing it.

Sounds simple, but most of us have developed a pretty strong override button that effectively silences our needs in one fell swoop, taking us out of any equation that comes up. Once our needs are cut off, we're no longer factored in. Instead, we move through the day on automatic pilot putting out fires, without regard to the inner yearnings of our souls.

CREATIVE STORY BY BARBARA MICHEL

"Recently while in the midst of a lot of life upheaval and transition, I rediscovered the powerful benefits of simply playing creatively. My husband and I were in the middle of a giant move and were not yet in our final home. The large majority of our belongings and all my art supplies were packed away for close to a year. It felt as if my artistic self was packed away as well. In addition, I was recovering from several large surgeries to repair my wrist after a bad accident. I needed some serious "art therapy" for sure! It felt daunting, but with a bit of effort, I created a small workspace and got my hands on some of my basic supplies.

I also decided to get myself a tool (new to me), called a "Gelli" plate. This is a reusable gel printing plate to use with water-based media, perfect for my medium of acrylics. I had no concrete goal in mind except to have some fun exploring some new techniques in color and texture and layering these on different kinds of paper. So as everyone knows who has used one of these, it is quickly addicting because it is so fun, and interesting results are immediate! I found myself spending many joyous hours in this new found creative exploration. I truly felt unleashed! I had no concern with the finished product, success or failure, only approaching each session with a "what if" attitude.

I realized how this playful attitude had been missing from my art time for too long! Gradually, I learned the effects I liked and didn't like, and began creating what I liked with conscious intent, as opposed to happy accidents. This eventually led to incorporating pieces of the printed papers into some small-scale collage pieces. The result feels like the beginnings of an exciting new direction for my work—I couldn't be more pleased.

We have now landed in our new home and are still settling in. There are many months of work ahead in this regard, but I have the memory of this wonderful experience well imprinted, and will not be waiting for all conditions to be just "perfect" before allowing myself the time and space to let loose and just play!

(Here are some questions Victoria posed to me about creative play:

What does creative play mean to me? To me, this means getting our heads (intellect) out of the process! Take the approach of pure exploration and "what if" in order to silence the inner critic and any expectations about a final result.

How is play a part of my creative process? Has it always been this way? Learning to adopt a playful attitude in my process has been a late in life "aha" for me. I am someone who has the tendency to take life and my art too seriously. I think this may stem from being forced at a young age to be an "adult" and having limited memories of joyful and free playtime. I am still learning how to make this an automatic part of my process. But one technique that has often been a great help is to start my painting session with an ugly duckling or unsuccessful painting. Here I can loosen up and try things with no risk. Sometimes covering over an entire painting with opaque paint, texturizing that layer while wet and exposing bits of what's underneath, can create an exciting new start of another painting. Other playful techniques I've used are (list to come).

Do artists tend to take themselves too seriously? How does this affect their art? I'm sure many artists have no issue with this at all, but I feel I might be a slow learner in this regard. I have evolved to more abstract and mixed media modes of painting over the years, and it is clear to me that too much seriousness is deadly in this style of painting.

It simply constricts the flow of creativity, which comes not from the head, but from within.

What can children teach us about creativity? *Creativity can be defined as the development of original ideas through exploration and discovery. If you watch children, you'll see their focus is all about their experiences with the process, without any concern at all with the final product or outcome. How delightful and liberating this is! My personal belief is that children are more closely connected to Spirit than adults, who have become more "polluted" with societal programming and the ego's agendas."*

LISTENING TO YOUR SOUL'S VOICE

People aren't mind readers. You must know what you want and ask for it. You must stake your claim or you will get walked on or, at least, left out. Yes, it's uncomfortable, but the juicy, creative part of life happens when we engage with it with our entire being.

WHAT DOES THIS LOOK LIKE?

- Asking for what you need
- Setting healthy boundaries with others
- Making time for regular self-care
- Eliminating negativity and hypercriticism
- Steeping out of your comfort zone and taking risks
- Putting fear in its place
- Listening to your intuition above ALL else

As you can certainly see, having a successful creative life requires that you have a healthy relationship with yourself. It sounds simple, however, don't be hard on yourself if you discover that you have a habit of ignoring your own needs. Many of us have had to face that head on when we decided to commit ourselves to expressing ourselves creatively.

Several years ago, I became aware of my own self-betrayal when a good friend offered to do a Feng Shui assessment of my home. After spending time walking through each room, examining the colors, the décor and the placement of furniture, she compiled her notes and shared her discoveries. At the time, I loved the artsy, colorful look and feel of this urban, two-story brownstone which was home to me, my husband, and our two sons. It came as quite a shock when my friend called me a few days later, and among other things, told me that the place was missing the energy of passion, and that try as she might, she couldn't find any evidence of me in the entire place. Instead, what was celebrated were the accomplishments and achievements of everyone else in my family.

I cried for a long time after that phone call. Then I walked around my beloved home and saw that she was right. I couldn't find myself there. In my emphasis on putting others' needs first, I'd rendered myself invisible, even in my own home. This was a potent wake-up call—a clear and undeniable truth that I could no longer ignore. If I didn't matter to myself, how could I expect anyone else to think I mattered?

Permission to love yourself means no more censoring yourself, no more holding back and no more second-guessing. It also means no more worrying about what other people think. Instead, create the space for the real you to emerge. Then, and only then, will you be free to love, and from that place, to receive and to give.

Question: What are three new ways that you can give yourself permission to love yourself?

Activity: Time to write another letter to yourself! This time I want you to focus on making a renewed commitment to honoring the sacred within yourself. I want you to be honest with yourself about the ways you are still holding back and not allowing yourself to feel loved by you and by the people in your life. Take some time to reflect and then answer the question: What do I need to feel loved right now? To take this a little further and begin to practice it with the people in your life. Begin to ask for what you need to feel loved. Then ask them what they need to feel loved. This practice can be transformational, however before you begin, explore the issue of love in your life with a letter.

Inspiration: Read *Love Yourself Like Your Life Depends On It* by Kamal Ravikant.

22
QUANTUM LEAPS OF BEING YOU

The privilege of a lifetime is to become who you truly are. — C.G. Jung

We have to dare to be ourselves, however frightening or strange that self may prove to be. — May Sarton

IN MY OWN PROCESS AS A WRITER, IT WAS THE DISCOVERY OF MY Muse that introduced me to the realm of the collective unconscious and the infinite well that we can draw on for creative ideas. What poured forth on the page was fresh, and most of it was a complete surprise to me. The ideas seemed to come from another realm, not simply from my own mind. I read them with awe and fascination as if I were reading something written by another person, not something coming through my own hands. I began to realize that what came from this deeper place was original and brand new, having never been born before. All I had to do was birth it into existence.

This experience is in stark contrast with what is created by the repetitive thinking of the mind. It's not difficult to see. In fact, there is so much imitation and rehashing of old ideas floating around in our world that when something original pops through, we all take notice. Why?

Because it feels different and because:
    it's refreshing, invigorating, and inspiring;
    it breaks all the previous rules;
    it changes the way we see things;
    it moves us in new directions;
    it opens up new possibilities;
    it's been sourced from this sacred wellspring.

This is where originality emerges—an otherworldly unknown place that we cannot see, touch or control. We can only tap into it through our willingness to work in partnership with the part of us that understands the language of that realm.

However, originality takes courage and requires that you risk failure, ridicule, and rejection. Most new ideas are laughed at when they're first brought forth. Some don't even come into full recognition until their originator is long gone.

Though it's not easy, it's well worth it. Over time, your work will gain in strength and accessibility. As you work with your Muse, your confidence in your own voice grows. Before long, it will become as familiar to you as your own body. You won't be looking around to see what others are doing or what they think, because you'll be so busy doing what you do and being you! Once you discover the beauty in that, the insecurity fades. It's a relief to finally, finally recognize that your instrument is meant to be tuned a specific way that is unique to you and no one else.

What matters is to continue to show up and fine-tune this

instrument. Before long you'll get so comfortable that you'll be bolder in your work, more vulnerable, and more real.

Of course, not everyone will love you. But that's okay. Enough people will receive something from you to inspire you to continue. This feedback loop will help to keep the momentum going and encourage you to take more and more steps into the realm of authenticity.

Being seen and loved as we are, is the ultimate reward for all our efforts. Doing less than we can do will leave us feeling dry and unfulfilled. Better to reach fewer people with something authentic, than to reach more with something we simply threw together with our skills.

People often make the mistake of doing something just because they're good at it. Skills are fine, but without passion and love for the process, it's an empty exercise with empty rewards. It's the difference between a meal cooked with love and one cooked without. The skills can be exactly same, but the one cooked with love will taste better. In fact, a meal cooked with love and less skill will still taste better than one cooked with more skill.

When someone is gifted in a specific area, the talent is strong enough that it almost appears second nature. Skills, on the other hand need to be mastered over time. While there can be a natural propensity to certain skills, gifts are deeply entrenched in a person's state of being.

Question: What makes your work unique in that it has a signature that shows it's yours and no one else's?
Activity: Write your creative manifesto. Ask yourself who you are and what you stand for. Use words to vividly express your values, burning convictions, passions, visions, beliefs, etc. Describe the ways in which your work is unique; describe its

essence, feeling, personality, tone, flavor and so on. If you're too close to it, ask your friends and loved ones to describe it for you. Take the words and sentences and make a list or design out of them. Get creative. Hang it where you can see it.

Inspiration: Do an online search for personal and creative manifestos.

23
SEIZE THE MOMENT

You must live in the present, launch yourself on every wave, find your eternity in each moment. Fools stand on their island of opportunities and look toward another land. There is no other land; there is no other life but this. — Henry David Thoreau

All that is important is this one moment in movement. Make the moment important, vital, and worth living. Do not let it slip away unnoticed and unused. — Martha Graham

NOT LONG AGO, I WAS CARRYING A VACUUM CLEANER DOWN A STEEP flight of stairs when I missed the bottom step, twisting my right ankle sideways. The pain was so severe for the first several minutes, I almost passed out. Later as I lay in bed icing my ankle, I realized I had not been present when I was walking down the stairs. My mind was racing around thinking about the list of things I wanted to get done that afternoon instead of where it needed to be: grounded in the moment. Though my ankle healed, I carry the experience with me as a reminder to slow down and keep my attention on what is happening right now.

The moment is all any of us have. Being present for it is our only way of truly living. Otherwise, we miss the precious gifts each one contains. In our daily lives, we're surrounded by opportunities all the time, but it takes a big dose of bravery to seize them. However, if we don't act, they will simply pass us by.

Living in the past or the future holds us hostage in that it removes us from the openings that happen when we're conscious and available. So often, we're so preoccupied with the ticker tape of thoughts running through our minds that we miss what's right in front of us.

Here's a story to illustrate:

SHEKH CHALLI

> "A rich man promised Shekh Challi (a poor man) some money if he would carry a pot of ghee for him. Shekh Challi agreed. He placed the pot on his head and followed his master. On the way, Shekh Challi pondered as to what he would do with his wages "I shall buy a goat with the money. Then, I'll start a small milk business. And with the profits I'll purchase a cow. With the money I make from its milk, I'll buy more cows. In no time I'll have a booming dairy business. Then, I'll have enough money to afford a nice home, get married and have kids. And when I am relaxing at home my son will come to call me for dinner. But I shall refuse."
>
> At this point Shekh Challi moved his head in refusal. The pot of ghee fell to the ground and broke spilling all the ghee on the ground. The master fumed with anger, "You've spilt my ghee you simpleton!"
>
> "But... you've only lost a pot of ghee and... I've lost a home, a wife and kids," replied Shekh Challi."

How can we practice being more present? Slowing down.

Listening with the heart and not the head. Tuning into our surroundings.

Easier said than done. Living amid a whirlwind of activity makes it seem impossible to even catch your breath, which is why it is necessary to become conscious of how much awareness you're losing when you aren't present. Awareness is half the battle. Then you can choose to practice bringing your attention back to the present.

The past and the future are alluring because they are composed completely of thoughts, and it's so easy to become lost there. They're both happening in your mind, whereas, the present is happening all around you. If you're in your head you're not here, and before long, even those moments will also be in your head.

The five senses are a good way to anchor your awareness to the present as is the breath. When you observe your mind taking off, notice your breath or the sensations of your five senses or even your emotions. Some of the other suggestions throughout the book can also help you stay focused on the present.

THE ENEMY OF DREAMS

Let's talk about the comfort zone. Comfort is the enemy of dreams. When comfort is your priority, comfort becomes your dream. Comfort is what you worship.

Comfort can make us passive and lead us to take the easy way. We get accustomed to the padded life and retreat when the edges get a bit sharp, and when there are disappointments. But it's part of the territory. To do anything worthwhile usually requires some compromise or sacrifice. It's not all going to be easy. The stories we love the most are the ones in which someone succeeds against the odds, they meet adversity head on and prevail, becoming stronger in the process. Comfort doesn't even factor into these stories. Instead, they involve lots of quick decisions made in the moment with no time to reflect, only the motivation of someone to act as best as they can.

CREATIVE STORY BY ROSSI DIMITROVA

"In my mid-twenties, I was convinced that I didn't have a creative bone in my body. I was working in finance, and my creativity was deeply buried.

Then one morning after a birthday, I woke up and knew I had to get a camera. I started photographing night scenes as a way of art therapy. I'd bring my tripod and camera to a quiet park, I'd click the button for a long exposure shot, and I would hear myself exhale.

With photography, I was able to become more present in the moment. I could feel the cold air and relax into it as opposed to running from it to a warmer place. I could hear the silence. Photography has become my way to tap into the flow of life. I experience it as an internal click - one moment I'd be stuck in my thoughts, and the next one a whole world of beauty opens before me.

Sunset lighting is my favorite. There is something very magical to me in sunset backlighting. I can see the simplest branch with leaves, and the lighting turns it into an exquisite scene that takes my breath away. Those flow moments are like a balm for my heart.

Nowadays in my work as a life coach, I experience bouts of the same kind of flow while I talk with clients. It is very exciting to me to discover a creative flow process in relating with others. It takes a level of commitment to the other person and a continuous deepening and discovery.

We are all complex beings and many times face difficult situations that don't have one pat solution. As a coach, for me to really assist another with their life dilemmas, I look to stay as present as I can and to listen deeply to what my heart is saying as I experience another person.

At one point a click happens, and an effortless insight emerges, and as I share it, I feel at peace, fearless, fully committed to the moment and to the truthful expression that's occurring. That flow experience is a little bit subtler than the photography one, but just as freeing."

People give up easily when discouraged or when setbacks happen. However, these challenges are essential—it is during these times that we learn where we are missing essential tools, resources, expertise, or the strength to fully hold the space for our dream. Typically, when we reach one level and are comfortable there, we are called to do something even bigger.

Life is about movement and change and growth. It's about showing up in the moment and seizing what is with open arms, knowing that it is exactly what we need to take us to the next step on our journey.

Question: What are you doing with the treasures life has given you?

Activity: Take another jar. Decorate it if you like and label it ACKNOWLEDGE. Take some small strips of paper that can easily be folded and write statements of appreciation for the blessings in your creative and personal life on them and put them into the jar.

Inspiration: Periodically pause, bringing your attention to the present moment and see what gifts, wisdom and inspiration naturally arise.

24

BECOME THE VESSEL

The truly creative mind in any field is no more than this: A human creature born abnormally, inhumanly sensitive. To him... a touch is a blow, a sound is a noise, a misfortune is a tragedy, a joy is an ecstasy, a friend is a lover, a lover is a god, and failure is death. Add to this cruelly delicate organism the overpowering necessity to create, create, create—so that without the creating of music or poetry or books or buildings or something of meaning, his very breath is cut off from him. He must create, must pour out creation. By some strange, unknown, inward urgency he is not really alive unless he is creating. — Pearl S. Buck

Neither a lofty degree of intelligence nor imagination nor both together go to the making of genius. Love, love, love, that is the soul of genius. — Wolfgang Amadeus Mozart

TO BECOME A VESSEL WITH WHICH TO HOLD YOUR GENIUS MEANS being open and empty so that you can receive and contain the flow of life energy that wants to be expressed through you. A vessel is a container; it holds whatever is poured into it until it is time to pour it out. When your Muse pours ideas into your vessel, you hold them until they are ready to be poured into a form and shared with the world.

Being able to hold big creative visions requires us to stretch and expand our capacity. This take practice. Otherwise, we'll find ourselves overwhelmed or burned by the intensity. Having a regular creative routine, rather than fits and starts or big periods of immersion, helps keep the flow moving without impediments or whitewater rushes of fear. Slow and steady, with lots of space, allows us to move beyond the boundaries of our comfort zones just enough to keep the energy fresh and alive.

Of course, making space means we must get out of our own way. Here's an excerpt from a blog post I wrote several years ago about this...

I once read that when Marlon Brando was asked why he didn't memorize his lines, he replied, "Real people don't know what they want to say." I relate to this because when I teach or give a presentation, it flows much better (and more authentically) when I don't prepare much beforehand. I can reflect on what I might like to do and have a few props handy, but the REAL stuff emerges when I get out of the way completely and just let what wants to come through flow unimpeded. Amazingly, I end up learning a hell of a lot as well.

After 18 years of teaching, I only discovered this recently when I began teaching teenagers. Knowing I needed to make my classes more dynamic and exciting to capture and sustain their attention, I accidentally stumbled upon a core truth at the heart of all creativity: THE LESS I TRIED to teach them or inspire them, the more I actually did, and THE MORE I TRIED, the more I failed. The juicy passionate fun stuff happens through you when you get out of the way. As soon as you put the "I" into the equation and try and manipulate the outcome, your efforts flatline and the passion gets sucked dry.

I shared this conversation in an email to my brother in-law, an artist, and he responded by describing his experience when he paints,

"When I go into a painting, you might say that I intend to be spontaneous once the brush has its first dip into the paint. When the painting is going well (here I begin to sound like Jackson Pollack) "I" have no idea of how it will go or come out. The more I try to intervene, the worse the result in the long run and "I" recognize it as a failure or simply as a bad result (since I'm an old hand at this). But then, I always hear the voice of Carl Sublett, one of my favorite professors, who said. "We never LOSE a painting," which means that your spontaneity can have freedom after you re-evaluate the painting and align yourself again with your original intention. You "repaint" the painting. In other words, it seems like intention is a program of the ego and spontaneity is when one releases oneself to that "cosmic intelligence" or "great spirit." "When the two are one, then you're on a roll."

I love his perspective there…the deep soulful wisdom that comes from painting for most of his life. Time and practice are great teachers with the biggest lesson being to surrender to the process, to stay open. It's humbling when we recognize how little control we really have over any of it—it's much bigger than we are.

In addition to surrender, being a vessel requires that you remove the debris and clutter from your head and your heart so that there's space for more of what brings you joy. This includes drama, worry, overindulgence, over-giving, over-doing, unnecessary distractions and time wasters, jealousy, resentment, self-doubt, passivity, and so on. Just imagine if even a couple of those things that take up space in your life were reduced significantly. What would you do with all that space?

When we create space in our heads and in our lives, there is more room for inspiration and ideas to shake us up, take us by surprise, and let us in on life's secrets.

Releasing oneself to that cosmic intelligence creates the space for magic to happen.

. . .

Life becomes more of a dance. Otherwise, creativity is just too much work and effort. Why would you want to paddle upstream when you can let go and allow the currents to take you downstream?

Question: How can you continue the process of emptying yourself, making space, opening your heart, and becoming the vessel for your Muse's creative ideas?
Activity: Using your RELEASE jar, write some things on small slips of paper that you still need to let go of to make more space in your life. They can be beliefs, concepts, physical possessions, commitments in your schedule, relationships, clients, habits, etc. Bless them and then contain them in this sacred jar.
Inspiration: Schedule mini-retreats in which the focus is on free-form, uninhibited in-the-flow creative expression. Instead of "making something happen" shift your view to "capturing the flow" that pours forth.

25
FATE AND DESTINY

I thought about one of my favorite Sufi poems, which says that God long ago drew a circle in the sand exactly around the spot where you are standing right now. I was never not coming here. This was never not going to happen. — Elizabeth Gilbert

DESTINY is a feeling you have that you know something about yourself nobody else does. The picture you have in your own mind of what you're about WILL COME TRUE. It's a kind of a thing you kind of have to keep to your own self, because it's a fragile feeling, and you put it out there, then someone will kill it. It's best to keep that all inside. — Bob Dylan

THE IDEAS OF FATE, DESTINY, CALLING, AND LIFE PURPOSE ARE fascinating to me, which is why I find the work of mythologists so enlightening. They use the language of metaphor, archetypes, and stories to reveal life's secrets and tell us about human existence. According to Michael Meade (whom I had the pleasure of hearing in person in 2011) storyteller, mythologist, and author of the book, *Fate & Destiny*, "Fate is the story of our lives unfolding from within us. When life is fully lived fate functions more as an oracle needing interpretation than a pre-determined outcome. Shifting fate and finding the destiny within it is part of the art of truly living and of living truly."

Another way to put it is this: If you see fate as what you're born into and destiny as what you make of that fate as you move through and interact with life, then you can use that perspective to illuminate the journey of your life.

Fate = our familial, ancestral, genetic, and environmental make up and circumstances.

Destiny = what we do with our fate and how we use it to create a life that is uniquely ours--that has our signature on it.

Meade suggests that we can break through the many limitations we were born with including "family history, a genetic predisposition, a specific fault, or an omission that wounds us" to find our destiny. These early constrictions are the cocoon around which we strengthen and build our character. It's where we learn what we're given and then challenged to transcend those limitations—rise above them or at the very least turn them into catalysts to propel us forward—and discover our soul's purpose.

Author S.L. Scott puts it more bluntly and less poetically. She writes, "Fate is the life you lead if you never put yourself in the path of greatness. That's the direction your life moves in without any effort on your part. That's your fate."

Ouch. Not a great way to live. Much better to focus on one's destiny.

She continues, "Destiny is your potential waiting to happen.

It's the top tier in the grand scheme of possibilities and where your dreams come true. You have to be willing to take that first step to reach your potential, even if it's a risk. With great risk comes great failure. Let's flip that phrase around. With great risk comes great reward. Ultimately, that means there's no greater risk than no risk at all."

For our purposes in this book, it would behoove us to cultivate a strong relationship with our Muse, so that we can make the most out of our fate, which will help us manifest our destiny. I would even go so far as to say *our Muse is the secret ingredient of a fully authentic life*. She holds the key that unlocks the door to our destiny. Without her help, we risk being bound by the limitations of our fate.

GIFTS & WOUNDS

Okay, but it's not always as easy as it sounds. So often life gets in the way or, as Meade points out, it's our wounds that get in the way. He says that each of us are born with a particular mix of gifts and wounds, and that we spend our lives learning how to work with what we've been given. Each highly impacts the other so that life becomes a dance of learning to carry the weight of these bequeathments.

Our gifts are our specific talents, strengths, passions, and inclinations. Our wounds, on the other hand, can show up as saboteurs of our gifts derailing us emotionally unless we learn to carry them: to heal what can be healed, integrate what can be integrated, and accept them as part of us. While our wounds make our lives challenging, they also build the character we need to carry our gifts; they add depth and universal beauty to our art.

Life is about walking with the grace and character to handle both our gifts and our wounds. It's a delicate balance that is helped greatly by solid, nourishing support and the recognition that the deepest realms of self-expression require a strong, healthy foundation.

This chapter is a big topic, and it's worth pausing to spend some time pondering this idea of your fate and your destiny to see what insights emerge. Here are some questions to help you explore this topic.

QUESTIONS

1. What are three gifts you have?
2. What are three wounds or inner saboteurs?
3. What is your destiny or life purpose?
4. What obstacles are currently in the way?
5. In what areas is your fate in the way of your destiny?
6. In what ways has your fate helped your destiny?
7. How can you strengthen your foundation and build your character so that you are better able to hold and carry your gifts and wounds?

Question: See above!
Activity: Answer the above list of questions in your CA journal.
Inspiration: Watch Michael Meade's "Purpose and Calling" video on You Tube.

PART VI

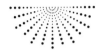

TRANSFORM YOUR LIFE

TRANSFORM YOUR LIFE

A hero ventures forth from the world of common day into a region of supernatural wonder: fabulous forces are there encountered and a decisive victory is won: the hero comes back from this mysterious adventure with the power to bestow boons on his fellow man. — Joseph Campbell

Sorrow prepares you for joy. It violently sweeps everything out of your house, so that new joy can find space to enter. It shakes the yellow leaves from the bough of your heart, so that fresh, green leaves can grow in their place. It pulls up the rotten roots, so that new roots hidden beneath have room to grow. Whatever sorrow shakes from your heart, far better things will take their place. — Rumi

As we enter the final section of this book, I'm sure you'll agree that creativity transforms lives. It performs alchemy in both our inner and our outer worlds, spreading its magic on everything and everyone it touches.

It's potent. It's mystical. It's catalytic.

As we plunge into the mystery of its power, we quickly discover that we need to cultivate the character to hold our creative gifts. We cannot tame the wilderness, we can only learn how to respectfully work with what we find there. This takes courage and practice, an open and trusting heart, along with a view that life and everyone in it is sacred, beginning with ourselves.

Learning to respect this journey and all that it entails ripens us, giving us the strength to show up when we're tired, to trust when we're full of self-doubt, and to persevere when we want to quit. This ability to become the container for our Muse so that she can do her work in, through, and around us, is one of the most profound of human experiences. It allows us to witness creation emanating from its primal roots, moving through the multitude of layers within until it finally emerges in all its messiness into the world of form where we'll shape it into something that can be shared with others.

This is co-creation my friends! It is our opportunity to enter the hinterlands of the eternal, nameless void out of which all that exists emerged. The seed and call to express ourselves this way planted deep into our hearts even before we ever touched solid ground. To deny its call is to deny our essence, the very substance of which drives our longing to belong, to connect, to contribute, and to love. We were born to share ourselves and it is through this giving that we utilize our gifts to create miracles and magic, to heal and uplift, to build and innovate.

Alas, it is so easy to forget these powers bestowed upon us or take them for granted. Thankfully, the world is full of mirrors and reminders—people who refuse to keep their song inside of them. These role models and mavericks cut the path for us so we won't be as afraid. "Come," they tell us, "The path is long and hard, but the bursts of joy you experience along the way are worth it."

Now that you've immersed yourself in the transformative juices of creativity, it's time to emerge from your protective inner sanctuary to enter the larger collective studio of the world. This section's topics are about connecting, collaborating, sharing your work, being of service, and keeping the faith.

REFLECTION QUESTION

How has creativity transformed your life?

BEFORE WE BEGIN

- Set an intention for this section.
- Spend some time reflecting on how creativity has transformed, healed, and enlivened your life. Write about it in your CA journal.
- Look at your three jars: RELEASE, CREATE, ACKNOWLEDGE. Create rituals to honor the contents. You may choose to bless them and burn them, recycle them, shred them or integrate them into your art. Whatever you decide, consciously be present for the ways in which these things you shared and contained served you in your life.

26
CREATIVE DATES

We have to continually be jumping off cliffs and developing our wings on the way down. — Kurt Vonnegut

There is a vitality, a life force, an energy, a quickening that is translated through you into action, and because there is only one of you in all time, this expression is unique. And if you block it, it will never exist through any other medium and will be lost. — Martha Graham

IN HER BESTSELLING BOOK, *THE ARTIST'S WAY*, JULIA CAMERON invites her readers to regularly make time for a creative field trip: an outing to an art gallery, museum or open mic. Artist dates can be a great way to get inspired so that you can return to your project with fresh eyes and energy.

Creative dates go a step further and move from inspiration to action. Creative dates are appointments you make with a creative friend or group of friends to get together and create! You can either work separately on your individual projects or you can collaborate on a project. The point is to set up specific times in which you hold yourself accountable to someone to spend some time doing something creative. What makes it especially appealing is that you aren't working alone!

I recommend arranging creative dates either once per week or at least once every other week, depending on how much accountability you need to accelerate your progress. The location can be varied. You can take turns working in each other's creative space, meet at a public space, or a combination of all three. The point is to add some spice to your creative process. Working with another person can stretch you in new ways, gifting you with new inspiration and growth.

Natalie Goldberg, in her book, *Writing Down the Bones*, wrote about meeting writing friends in cafes so that both would feel inspired to write at a set time. As I mentioned earlier, I wrote my first full-length screenplay in a café across the street from my apartment. When I hit a creative road block, I'd ask the owner of the café—also a screenwriter—for help. His response was always the same: "just get it down". That simple advice helped me push through the resistance I encountered working in a new format. I was afraid I'd do it wrong or badly. My perfectionism was getting my way. Fortunately, because I was in an environment with another screenwriter, he helped me trust the process so I would keep going.

The nasty negative gremlins also tend to be worse when you're alone. If you find yourself feeling particularly down and defeated, creative dates can change things up or at least, shift your energy. I've organized creative dates in my home, and really thrived on the energy of a group of people engaging with the Muse at the same time.

COLLABORATION

In addition to the accountability benefits of collaboration, it's also another great way to get motivated when you find yourself in a slump or not as passionate about your own creative projects. The collective energy of two or more people adds lots of interesting ideas to the mix, elevating the project to a completely different level than it would have been had it been completed by one person. Sometimes you can return to your own solitary projects rejuvenated and ready to re-engage.

As you've probably gathered reading this book, many of the suggestions to help you become more creative are, in a sense, a way to outsmart the reasoning mind so that you can slip past the gates of resistance. Perhaps you will eventually find a rhythm and you won't need any of these tricks. However, it's nice to know these tricks are there when you need them, especially when you're feeling stuck.

SUGGESTIONS FOR CREATIVE DATES

- Host a creative date at your home or studio for creative friends.
- Meet a creative buddy once a week in a cafe or online via Skype.
- Collaborate on a creative project with one or more friends either locally or remotely and regularly meet to share progress and ideas.
- Arrange to do weekly or bi-weekly artist dates with a friend. Go to places that inspire you and nourish your creativity: bookstores, galleries, museums, open mics, etc., and then plan to do something creative of your own afterwards.

- Gather people together to do art and then give the art you create away to strangers.
- Host a doodling party.
- Host a writing prompt party.

Question: How can creative dates positively impact your creative life?

Activity: Set up a creative date with a creative buddy or a group of creative friends. It can be as simple as you like. Make it fun and something you would look forward to. See it as another way of loving yourself and finding your voice.

Inspiration: Visit the Indie Kindred website and watch *Indie Kindred* movie.

27
CREATIVE COMMUNITY

A tribe is a group of people connected to one another, connected to a leader, and connected to an idea. For millions of years, human beings have been part of one tribe or another. A group needs only two things to be a tribe: a shared interest and a way to communicate. — Seth Godin

Circle is not anything new. Circle is an ancient process of consultation and communion, a place for slowing down, respectfully listening and being heard, a place to change the conversation and a way of being together that taps into the deep well of wisdom and creative thinking that is so needed in this time and place in history. Being in Circle is a matter of remembering our original way of being in community. — Birute Regine, author of *Iron Butterflies: Women Transforming Themselves and the World*

MY FIRST WRITING GROUP, MOTHERS WHO WRITE, BEGAN WITH around eight women. This was before the internet and social media. I placed a small one-paragraph ad in the monthly newsletter of a popular Minneapolis writing center called "The Loft". It struck a nerve. Mothers from all around the Minneapolis area (where I lived at the time) began calling me excited and grateful that I was starting such a group. I received over forty phone calls within the first week. Within two weeks, we had our first meeting. I was so nervous! I served tea and muffins, but no one touched the food—not because they weren't hungry, but because they were too excited by the opportunity to focus on their writing, they didn't care about the food! We met twice a month for two hours on Saturday mornings for a year until I moved back east to New Jersey, where I'm from. I learned so much that year: I wrote more, got a few things published, and felt much more confident as a writer. But more than that, I learned what the power of a group could do for the individual members within it. Something about the encircling energy and the way it contains the members sparks a kind of synchronistic flow that opens people up and makes them braver and more willing to jump into places they wouldn't touch on their own.

After I moved, the women in the group decided to continue meeting as a group, and I decided to start a brand new one in my new home. I was onto something and I didn't want to let it go. Apparently neither did they. The group eventually became known as *Women Who Write* when a friend of mine, childless and unmarried at the time, wanted to join. Over time, that group expanded and grew into ten groups with over 100 members.

This was just the beginning. From there, I started a hugely successful monthly writer's salon that ended up being sponsored by a library and averaged 20-40 attendees per month. We had guest speakers (a literary agent, an intellectual property attorney, a published author), we did public readings and we discussed everything related to the writer's life. We had a blast! I also ran a monthly women's discussion group. All three groups attracted the attention of the local press and all three groups opened big, huge doors in my life that have been evolving ever since.

A community of kindred spirits that support you on your creative journey is one of the best ways to achieve consistency and sustainability as you evolve in your process. I cannot recommend it enough! One thing I learned over the years is this:

Without the ongoing regular support of a group of people, it is extremely difficult to experience a high quality of life.

Because we feel supported, groups can inspire us to overcome fear, take risks, and get out of our comfort zones. This extends beyond the group meetings to such an extent that even if we're not with the group members every day, we can still feel their presence moving with us through our lives—kind of an invisible, but powerful lifeline that's always present. This was true with that first writing group. Even though we only met twice a month, I could feel the energy of my group as I wrote and submitted my work to publishers. I found myself not only more productive in my writing, but also more willing to stretch because I was surrounded by the force field of the other women writers who cared what happened to me. I never forgot that feeling. To this day, I'm eternally grateful to that first group for revealing this powerful resource to me.

A SACRED CONTAINER

When you gather a group of kindred spirits together, you create a sacred container in which something magical happens: *that circle of people ends up being something greater than the sum of its parts.* A powerful, dynamic energy emerges from the group collective and it opens a channel to the even greater collective of life. All the content, energy, tools, inspiration, information, insights and resources—everything that's needed becomes accessible in that context. Because of that, people can share great levels of wisdom, to become vulnerable with each other and to establish a higher level of trust than they would in a typical social setting. This fosters a deep level of intimacy with people who barely know each other very quickly. It also draws out different levels of motivation, honesty, healing, growth, and learning Sharing stories can motivate people to take an action that they might not otherwise. When someone models something new, it gives people the courage to step out of their comfort zones.

THE MANY GIFTS OF GROUP EXPERIENCE

- Shared experiences
- A context that encourages service to others, thinking of someone other than oneself
- Inspiration and encouragement
- Information
- Modeling behavior and social skills
- Stories
- Healing due to a feeling of belonging
- Self-responsibility and honesty
- Self-awareness and understanding

A NEW DOOR OF POSSIBILITY

In a group environment, the potential to shift expands within people when they see they're not alone. Seeing that others are facing similar fears and challenges creates a feeling of relief. Hearing someone say, "Here's what I'm going to do about that...." or "Here's what I did about that..." it's as if someone opens a new door of possibility, stirring people who may have been frozen or immobile for months, or even years.

I encourage you to run—don't walk—to your nearest creative group, and if you can't find one, start one! That's what I did, and I promise, you won't regret it!

We cannot do this alone.

We cannot do this overnight.

We cannot do this by reading about it.

We need the ongoing regular support of a group of people invested in each other's wellbeing.

∾

Question: Do you currently have the support you need in your creative life?
Activity: Examine your life and see if having the support of a creative group would help you. By this I don't mean e-courses or online groups. Instead, I'm referring to an actual group of creative buddies that will become your greatest allies and advocates as you navigate through the creative wilderness. It can make a HUGE difference in your life and is another form of self-love to nurture and care for yourself this way. Life is hard enough, so why traverse it alone, when you could surround yourself with others who care about your well-being and creative progress.
Inspiration: Read *The Artist's Way* by Julia Cameron.

28
SHARING YOUR WORK

Creative work is not a selfish act or a bid for attention on the part of the actor. It's a gift to the world and every being in it. Don't cheat us of your contribution. Give us what you've got. — Steven Pressfield

Thousands of candles can be lit from a single candle, and the life of the candle will not be shortened. Happiness never decreases by being shared. — Buddha

SHARING YOUR WORK IS A BRAVE AND VULNERABLE LEAP ON THE creative path. It's also one of the most rewarding things you can do. I consider it "coming out of the closet" because you're finally outing (and owning) yourself as a creative person—that, more than the actual sharing is what makes it so profound, and also what makes it feel so big and terrifying.

The first leap for me was sharing my writing with my small writing group. During our first few meetings, I noticed a trend with the women. Right before they shared a story, essay or poem, they timidly looked around and apologized in advance that the writing might not be any good. I put a stop to that right away. No apologies allowed! Just dive in and read! It helped that I told everyone that it was optional to ask for feedback, and if they did ask, they could tell us to be gentle or to focus on one specific aspect of the writing. Whew! I saw relief on their faces. This is where I first learned the importance of baby steps. Never push. Never force. And never, ever crush the heart of an open, vulnerable writer who is stepping out of the creative closet for the very first time. It happened to me once in one of my own groups. That's when I instituted guidelines. Never again did I want writers in one of my groups to feel discouraged about writing.

Another big coming out for me occurred when I read one of my short stories for the first time at a public reading. It was an event put on by a fiction-reading group I'd joined months before. Being part of a group helped, but knowing there was a reporter in the audience added to the intense pressure I felt. Thankfully, I'd been reading my writing to my writing group members for a couple of years prior to this event. It was another in a series of bold moves that grounded me firmly in the domain of seeing myself as a writer. It was exhilarating and terrifying at the same time.

Sharing your work is a great context in which to find your creative voice. It's an ideal opportunity to view it with fresh eyes and see if it still resonates with your vision of what you want to be putting out into the world.

CREATIVE STORY BY JENNIFER MAGEL

"During the months of February and March of 2014, I showed my work at a gallery and coffee shop at Pike Place Market. Despite my

considerable nervousness, the opening went well and my work was very well received. It's an interesting situation to be standing there in front of your work- almost like you are on display yourself. As someone who doesn't feel very outgoing, it's a challenge to put yourself out there and open yourself up to criticism, judgment—and really for most of us who are creative—really showing people who we are through our art.

I was discussing this with one of my fellow featured artists at the opening and she said, "Really, we're showing our hearts and our souls out here—a lot of people don't get that!" It was refreshing to hear that she had the same take on exhibiting her artwork and could relate to the feelings I was having. I felt less alone and more a part of a group of people who sing their song through their creative pursuits—identifying themselves through their art.

This past summer, I showed my work in New York City at a one-night event in Lower Manhattan. I was a bit of a mess heading into that morning to hang the work and prep it for the show that evening. As I walked from my hotel to the venue I looked around at all the hundreds of people on the streets bustling around me, and I thought "Look at me, I've chosen to be very brave and share my work with potentially ANY of these people. They all have an opportunity to judge me on the streets right now, but at my show I will metaphorically undress and show them the core of who I am. This is scary. But I feel SO alive! This is amazing! This is what it is to be truly living!"

Charged with the adrenaline of fear and nerves, I had to fight the fear and just move into the experience of it. And it was beautiful. People were very curious and complimentary. I also had the first big sale of my career at that show. Looking back at it now, I am so proud of myself for stepping towards the challenges, feeling the discomfort and DOING IT ANYWAY. That's the thing—sometimes we forget what it feels like to be truly alive until we have our hearts beating the hell out of us in our chests and our nerves are lit up like the 4th of July. Coasting on that wave and riding it out to the end is the reward because as we've opened up to others, we've grown. And we look over our shoulders and realize that we now have wings to fly, making the next adventure or challenge that much easier."

There are many ways to share your work. It's important to gauge your own level of vulnerability with it, and also to know when and where to share it. But don't be afraid to stretch a bit out of your comfort zone from time to time. There are small venues and there are big ones. There are local, little-known open mics if you're looking to perform or cafes if you want to show your work. Contests are a great option if you'd prefer to play it a bit safe. You can also shoot for something bigger. You have nothing to lose. However, if you're sensitive to rejection, don't raise the bar too high—you don't want to risk feeling heart-broken coming right out of the gate.

I used to take rejection personally until it happened enough times for me to learn that it's simply part of the process. Then, when I did get published, I realized how random and subjective the whole thing is, making it easier to stop linking my well-being to how much people liked or didn't like my creative work. Instead, I focused on how much joy I received just from immersing myself in the process. That was enough.

Sharing is extra, and it flows better if it comes not from an ego need to receive validation, but rather from a genuine desire to share unconditionally and give others the joy of experiencing your work.

Question: Is it time to share your creative work with the world?
Activity: Create a goal for some time this year to share your work in a way that is brand new for you, either because it's the first time you've shared your work (or shared your work in a

long while), OR it's out of your comfort zone, OR it's the first time you've collaborated with someone, OR you're working in a brand new medium or venue OR you're exposing yourself to a MUCH bigger audience than ever before. If any of that sounds too overwhelming, then just set a small goal that's a baby step from where you are now. Do a little something different in terms of sharing your work. It could be gifting someone with some of your art or leaving some of it to be found be others. Anything will work as long as it stretches you a bit.

Inspiration: Read *Share Your Work: 10 Ways to Share Your Creativity and Get Discovered* by Austin Kleon.

29
SERVICE TO OTHERS

I slept and dreamt that life was joy. I awoke and saw that life was service. I acted and behold, service was joy. — Rabindranath Tagore

The purpose of life is not to be happy. It is to be useful, to be honorable, to be compassionate, to have it make some difference that you have lived and lived well. — Ralph Waldo Emerson

MANY OF US WERE RAISED TO VIEW CREATIVITY AS FRIVOLOUS, indulgent, and even selfish. However, it is, in fact, one of the least selfish things we can do with our lives. Please don't underestimate that. Sharing our gifts and our unique way of seeing the world can be uplifting, enlightening, inspiring, healing, and simply joyful to anyone who experiences it. Imagine the world without any form of artistic expression and you'll appreciate what I mean.

But there is more we can do. Once we establish a strong creative habit and get into a regular flow with our creativity, it is a natural next step for us to assist those around us who are finding it difficult to do the same. Lighting the creative fire in another is extremely rewarding.

There are several ways you can do this:

1. Start a creative circle or Meetup group
2. Organize an open mic at a local café or bar
3. Mentor a young person
4. Volunteer to teach at a local community center, prison or nursing home
5. Start a blog about the creative process
6. Offer free webinars or in person presentations at the library
7. Donate some of your work to raise money for a fundraiser for a local charity
8. Bring art to impoverished communities

Some artists combine their creativity with their passion for activism. They use it to bring awareness to others about injustice or poverty. There are hundreds of examples of this and it's a highly effective way of delivering a message.

Others spend time bringing art to people who otherwise wouldn't have access to it. It's a way to expand the reach of art into the smaller, less visible, often neglected nooks and crannies of life and contributes greatly to the well-being of others.

Being a role model for younger generations is another powerful way to plant seeds for future generations. This is especially important since so many arts programs have lost their funding and been cut from school budgets.

It's amazing how creativity can be such a light in the world. I liken the path of the artist with the path of the mystic. I trust you'll agree when you read Jacqueline Small's definition of mystic:

> "Mystics are born, they are not created. People recognize themselves as mystics when they remember that all of their lives, they have known there is something much grander going on here than is obvious. Mystics are born knowing that life is purposeful and that humans are both human and divine. In times past, mystics were considered impractical because they were dreamers, visionaries who could see the future and understood what humanity was trying to accomplish. However, they usually were quiet and not activists. The archetype currently coming through human consciousness is the practical mystic, which is not just a seer of Spirit's work, but a doer of Spirit's work."

Creative artists are essentially practical mystics in that they see themselves with the grander purpose of being an intermediary between the formless and the world of form. We're interpreters of the language of the mysteries and secrets of the collective unconscious. We mine for these subterranean gifts and present them with our own signature on them.

It takes vulnerability and bravery to risk entering these formless realms; we also risk disappointment that our efforts will not meet our standards and rejection because others may not accept our efforts. However, the desire to contribute something meaningful to the world, helps many of us move past these risks. We carry on trusting that someone may benefit.

Our work is not for us alone. It is our way of giving back. When I learned to write, I longed to give back, creating books that would touch others in the ways that I had been touched.

Marketing guru, Seth Godin has been claiming for years that art is going to save the world. I couldn't agree more. It's universal right-brained language that crosses cultures, borders, and language barriers with a common message shared by all humans —a message that can only be found in the heart: love.

Question: How can you be of service to others using your creativity? If you're already doing that, what can you do to expand that?

Activity: Make a commitment to find a new way of being of service to others using your creativity. Listen, follow your heart and go with what resonates. Do what is authentic and realistic within the parameters of your current life. It doesn't have to be big, but perhaps it could be something that makes you stretch a bit. The point is to create a circle of giving and receiving such that the two become indistinguishable. Therein lies the ultimate alchemy of creativity and its real transformative power.

Inspiration: Watch *Opening Our Eyes* movie.

30
KEEPING THE FAITH

KEEPING THE FAITH

None of us knows what might happen even the next minute, yet still we go forward. Because we trust. Because we have Faith.
— Paulo Coelho

Nature loves courage. You make the commitment and nature will respond to that commitment by removing impossible obstacles. Dream the impossible dream and the world will not grind you under, it will lift you up. This is the trick. This is what all these teachers and philosophers who really counted, who really touched the alchemical gold, this is what they understood. This is the shamanic dance in the waterfall. This is how magic is done. By hurling yourself into the abyss and discovering its a feather bed. — Terrence McKenna

SEVERAL YEARS AGO, A THERAPIST FRIEND POINTED OUT THAT MANY people frequently devoted themselves only 75% to a new project or followed a path only three quarters of the way, and then quit, never waiting long enough to see anything through to the finish.

This is not uncommon; 12-step members refer to it as, "quitting before the miracle".

When the going gets tough, most of us quit and try something else. It's easy to enjoy the beginning of something—the excitement of a new project, a new town, a new job is exhilarating. It gives us a tremendous amount of energy. Most of us believe the newness will last, and that we'll be able to sustain our enthusiasm. But it never does. Once the newness wears off, it can be challenging to sustain our interest and investment, making us long to move on.

It's akin to the romantic phase of a relationship, when everything is seen through rose-colored glasses—full of the magical glow of hope and promise. In a new creative project, we're in love with our ideas. Our expectations run high. We think this new project will somehow have the power to lift us out of our current limited state to soar to epic heights of grandeur. It can, and it sometime does, but not usually to the level our minds think it will.

Reality sets in. All our old habits are still there, our bodies look the same and we don't feel exhilarated at every turn like we thought we would. But that's okay. No one can burn at that high rate for too long, or we'd burn out.

Not seeing something through, unfortunately, results in a multitude of unfinished business. Half-baked ideas and projects lie around defeated by the specter of impatience. We envy others who have completed major works, who have stuck with something long enough to see improvement and some level of success. We want success to sneak up on us and surprise us while we're not looking.

Alas, success doesn't work that way. Thank goodness it doesn't, because without the hard work and sense of accomplishment from something well done, success wouldn't be worthwhile. It would simply be another empty shell of something that only resembled happiness.

It reminds me of the saying, "God is in the details". It's the journey—all the steps along the way that are important. When you're too busy (or too successful) you don't stop to notice these details, and large chunks of life zoom by. All the striving and effort to achieve a goal is worthless unless it is done in a sane and meaningful way, with attention to the details.

Life is a cycle of highs and lows, ups and downs. Inspiration is a necessary aspect of any project, but it is only a very small part of it. Anyone who has achieved any degree of success knows that it is the willingness to see something through which leads one to the realm of success.

George Leonard, in his book, *Mastery*, examines the process one goes through to master a new set of skills. It is a process of ebbs and flows, which he dubs, "The Mastery Curve". He writes, "Learning any new skill involves relatively brief spurts of progress, each of which is followed by a slight decline to a plateau somewhat higher in most cases than that which preceded it."

It is the long plateaus of seemingly no progress, which lead many people to give up. They get bored or frustrated, and therefore, are no longer inclined to continue along the road to true mastery. Instead, they settle. Satisfied that they've put in enough effort, they simply rest on the little bit of success they've achieved.

But true mastery means going all the way with something, continually improving, continually innovating, and continually practicing without end. The result is that you've not only mastered something, but you've succeeded in achieving a goal. This requires persistence, patience, and a passion for the process. In other words, you've got to love what you're doing or you'll never be able to make it through the rough spots. As Leonard puts it, "You practice diligently but you practice primarily for the sake of the practice itself."

CREATIVE STORY BY REBECCA CAVENDAR

The candles are lit.

The incense is burning.

Oil is placed in the palm of my hands, kissing my third eye, my crown.

Here, I begin to breathe.

With a hand on my heart, I connect to sacred stillness.

In an act of loving surrender, of trust, I let go of my mind.

It is not about me.

It is about listening.

Breathing, waiting, releasing.

Emptying.

The Muse transforms the busy-ness of my life, my mind, my fears into acceptance.

A hush comes over me, silent, a dream-like honeyed state.

Sweet and slow.
In this stillness, I know I am not alone.

In between worlds, I ask for guidance. A passage in a book, an image on an oracle card, or words whispered in my ear, tracing my spine. Bring awareness and reveal connection so I can weave new words, a new story, a new dream.

The subject I will write about is clear; ritual provides the transcendent space and inspiration on how to write about it.

All of creating is holy.

All of creating is sanctified when blessed with the freedom to express what is true.

A spacious resonance is created.

The quintessence of what wants to come through, what wants to be shared takes form in my mouth. Words move down my arms, through my fingers, out the pen.

My job is to breathe. To listen. To trust.

Perhaps the words are for a client. Maybe the public.

Sometimes, it is just for me to process what is aching in my bones.

Regardless of audience, there is a responsibility to create a piece that sensitively and vulnerably inspires, uplifts.

Intuition guides.

Intuition releases me from the burden of having to find the perfect words.

Intuition releases me of having to BE perfect, to do it all on my own.

This is the alchemy of ritual and intuitive writing.

It is about getting out of you own way so that you can be of service.

It is about being a vessel.

It is about love.

~

Keeping the faith and hanging in there when the going gets tough—that's what makes all the difference. Perhaps if we knew how hard something was going to be, how long it would take or how many obstacles we'd meet along the way, we'd never even begin. But good ideas are hard to ignore. There is something in the human heart that longs to express itself. It is this tremendous need to create and contribute, which leads to the entire myriad of new inventions and information flooding our lives every day.

When you give something your "all" you are rewarded in kind with the gift of self-fulfillment. There are few things in this world that are worth more than that. In all your striving, and forward-thinking motions, what keeps you sane is that you finally feel as though you're on the right track. It's as though this path has been there all along and you've finally found it.

Success has a price. It takes guts, perseverance, and a strong vision. It takes an unfailing belief in oneself, and in one's ability to beat the odds. It takes a willingness to keep going no matter how hard or bumpy the road becomes, or how many detours crop up along the way. The price tag is big, but the rewards are even bigger. And getting there is half the fun.

It's like coming home. Suddenly all other roads look foreign, and you cannot imagine doing anything else, and you wonder how you put up with the detours and wrong directions for so long. But now you're on your way, and no matter what happens, you know you've connected with an eternal flame that resides within you that you carry forever in your heart.

Question: If, with a wave of a magic wand, all your fear and resistance were suddenly replaced by faith and trust, what would you do?
Activity: Take some baby steps toward one of your biggest dreams. Just a few. Nothing scary or major. But do take them. Notice how you feel. Let that feeling wash over you and use it to propel you forward until you feel like taking some more baby steps. Many baby steps add up to big steps, but they're easier to take and less noticeable. So, get in there and start to make things happen. Don't hold back anymore waiting for the right time.
Inspiration: Explore The Alliance of Artists Communities website—a listing of residencies, communities, colonies, retreats, workspaces, and studio collectives.

CONCLUSION

IN CLOSING OUR JOURNEY TOGETHER, I BOW TO YOU AND YOUR Muse in gratitude for taking this sacred journey with me at this time in your life. None of us should take this trek through the inner wilderness alone. Having a guide light our way makes it easier to see and even trust the process more.

As you take what you've learned here—process it, own it, and integrate it into your own learning pathways, observe the subtle changes that are unfolding. Listen to the whispers that are arising as your soul steps out from behind the curtain into the beautiful nakedness of your authentic Creative Self.

Don't hesitate here. Now is not the time to hold back or withdraw into the familiar comfort zone. Instead, embrace the uncertainty. Test the waters. Find your footing. And when you're feeling shaky, flip through the pages of this book or your journal and remind yourself of what you already know, and then step forward with confidence in the direction of your sacred creative expression. Give it all you've got and let yourself free fall into the bliss of the Real.

This is your time to shine! Don't let it pass you by! Life passes in the blink of an eye and you must grab it and go like the wind.

There is no tomorrow waiting for you with open arms, there is only now embracing you right here, imbuing you with the courage to let the beauty flow out from the deep well inside you out into this world.

You are needed. So, get going....

ABOUT THE AUTHOR

Victoria Fann is a writer, transformational coach, community builder and practical mystic. The foundation of her work was inspired by her time at Esalen Institute, as well as her training and inner work with many of the early founders and teachers of the human potential movement. She's been writing essays, short stories, plays and screenplays for over three decades. Her writing has been published in numerous publications and anthologies including Women of Wisdom, Newsweek, Thought Catalog, Elephant Journal, Wake Up World, Snapping Twig, Medium, BioStories, etc. You can read more of her writing and learn more about her on her website www.victoriafann.com.

CREATIVE STORY CONTRIBUTORS

Rebecca Cavender is a best-selling, professional intuitive writer from the Pacific Northwest. She writes lyrical words to catalyze sacred self-expression in others as well as in herself. www.rebeccacavender.com

Tanya Cole is a contemporary painter who possesses a passionate focus in portraying people and nature to uplift, reflect and inspire the human spirit. Playing and experimenting with tonal variation, texture and colour to evoke different mood and emotion; her paintings open us up to feel and deeply connect consciously with our selves through opened and awakened senses. https://tanyacolearts.com/

Shari Killian Daniels is an assistant professor at the University of Minnesota-Crookston, as well as a literacy coach, blogger, writer, artist and photographer . She offers online writing courses and is deeply inspired to help others know that they matter. https://islandsofmysoul.com/

Rossi Dimitrova is an Authentic Relating and Circling facilitator, ecstatic dancer and lover of all that is true and alive. She published her *Free Hugs* book and started an Authentic Relating community in Chicago in 2016 and aims to create spaces where humans feel comfortable to truly be themselves. www.rossijoyphoto.com

Sandy King defines her art as one that reflects the space behind and within a narrative, regardless of the tools she hold in her hands. She sees life through the eye of a jester, and is always looking for a thread of humour. www.sandymairart.com

Liz Labunski is a mixed media artist who primarily works with acrylic paint, collage, and watercolor. She has also spent several years of her creative journey exploring jewelry making. https://labunskistudio.com/

Jennifer Magel is an artist, designer and maker. Always tenacious about creativity, she continues to pursue her passion of making art and teaching others to connect with their inherent creativity! www.indelibleinkcreative.com

Suzanne McRae is a writer and abstract artist who often finds her creative expression coming from the depths of her inner world and her life experiences. In her art and writing she uses colours and symbols, insights and wisdom to help others discover a richer and deeper connection to who they truly are. www.suzanne-mcrae.com

Barbara Michel has been drawing and painting as long as she can remember, and in an earlier chapter of life, was shown widely in the Washington, DC area where she resided. She currently is a full time caregiver to her husband, but is exploring more intuitive and playful approaches to her work, which is her

CREATIVE STORY CONTRIBUTORS

therapeutic "soul work". She can be reached at barbara826@gmail.com.

Suzi Poland is an artist, designer and dreamer, whose work in a variety of mediums traverses the space between the real and imagined, functional and aesthetic, personal and public. She is inspired by nature, the seasons and the world around her as much as by her own emotional landscape and loves creating joyous, illustrative, whimsical art for all ages that can be given as gifts or other occasions. www.suzipoland.com

Andrea Saccone Snyder is a mixed media artist, author of *The Mindful Beauty Makers Little Book Of Wisdom* and the founder of The FLOW Beauty Project, which empowers salon professionals to nurture their inner beauty while reclaiming their most creative selves. www.theflowbeautyproject.com

Sarah Spector is a lifelong artist and painter. She also plays several instruments, sings, and works as a healer and clairvoyant. www.sarahspector.com

Made in the USA
Middletown, DE
19 May 2019